With wisdom, candor, and great self-awareness, Nanci Shanderá writes beautifully of the importance of complete self-acceptance. And in this she is right: there is no greater lesson for those of us here on the Earth plane. In this richly insightful book, she skillfully and lovingly shows us how to master this lesson.

—Robert Schwartz, award-winning author of *Your Soul's Plan: Discovering the Real Meaning of the Life You Planned Before You Were Born*

Your Inner Gold is a deep, comprehensive guide to attaining our intrinsic wholeness. Dr. Shanderá shares the wisdom and tools necessary for transformation in a profound and engaging way. This is the best spiritual book I've seen in many years!

—Carolyn Conger, PhD, psycho-spiritual teacher and consultant

In *Your Inner Gold*, Nanci Shanderá guides us through a journey from the surface of our skin, to our bones, to our Diamond Soul, and back out again into our love and service for the World! Through personal story and offerings from various healing traditions, Nanci's writing inspires, guides, nudges, and nurtures the song of soul transformation that is at the core of our heart's longing.

—Sanchi Reta Lawler, Zen Buddhist teacher and Transformative Guide

Your Inner Gold is a very useful guide and consistent encouragement for people to look beyond their ego-identified selves, to the potential for freedom and a greater identification with the divine. There are many examples of openings to higher understanding and great exercises to tweak the reader's thinking out of the box. Dr. Shanderá has written openly and generously about this process and is navigating a complicated and interesting road—both assimilating others' work and deepening a theory for understanding Soul. The reader will find permission to accept the human self with its bumps and bruises, while exploring and finding the true spiritual self.

—Valerie Kack, PhD, LCSW, psychotherapist, artist, and author of *The Emotion Handbook for the Recovery and Management of Feelings*

YOUR
INNER
Gold

© Ashley Shanderá

About the Author

Dr. Nanci Shanderá is the director of EarthSpirit Center for the Transformational Arts in Nevada City, CA. Formerly, as a Religious Science minister, she administered the Ernest Holmes College School of Ministry in Los Angeles, where she also taught transformational intensives. She draws from over thirty years experience in nontraditional spiritual teaching and counseling. She has written a transformational novel entitled *The Quilt: A Woman's Journey to Power,* and is currently preparing notes and planning interviews for a book titled *The Elder Heroine's Journey,* which explores how women age and can become the Wise Women of our global tribe. She invites you to "Like" her business page, EarthSpirit Center, on Facebook.

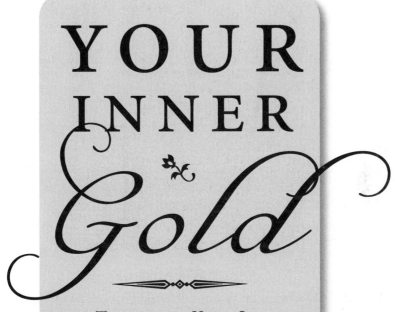

YOUR INNER *Gold*

TRANSFORM YOUR LIFE
AND
DISCOVER YOUR SOUL'S PURPOSE

NANCI SHANDERÁ, PhD

Llewellyn Publications
Woodbury, Minnesota

FIRST EDITION
First Printing, 2013

Book design by Donna Burch
Cover art: Gold retro background on cover and paisley pattern on back cover:
        iStockphoto.com/ShutterWorx
Cover design by Ellen Lawson
Editing by Andrea Neff

Llewellyn Publications is a registered trademark of Llewellyn Worldwide Ltd.

Library of Congress Cataloging-in-Publication Data
Shanderá, Nanci.
  Your inner gold : transform your life and discover your soul's purpose / by Nanci
Shanderà, PhD.—First Edition.
      pages cm
  Includes bibliographical references and index.
  ISBN 978-0-7387-3335-7
1. Spiritual life. 2. Alchemy—Religious aspects. I. Title.
  BL624.S47645 2013
  204'.4—dc23
                                                                    2013001263

Llewellyn Publications
A Division of Llewellyn Worldwide Ltd.
2143 Wooddale Drive
Woodbury, MN 55125-2989
www.llewellyn.com

Printed in the United States of America

For Brugh, profound and eternal teacher,
with a heart of gratitude.

For my mother, June Gooch Leland,
with love and thanks for completing the agreement.

For my daughters, Seana and Ashley,
and my incredible grandchildren,
with unending love.

Contents

Acknowledgments

So many thanks to so many people! This book could not have been published without the help of the following people.

First and foremost, I owe my daughter Ashley, who is a writer herself, a great debt of thanks for all her assistance in so many ways in the process of putting this book together. I am grateful to all of my students through the years for sharing their deep and meaningful processes, from which I learned much. Special thanks go to Rev. Sallie Kinard for her very helpful comments in the draft stage, LuAnne Myers for her all-around support, Dr. Valerie Kack for having helped me to polish this work, and to Robert Schwartz for his support of a fellow author! I want to especially thank Dennis William Hauck, who set me on this incredible alchemical pathway many years ago.

I feel particularly fortunate in working with my extraordinary editor, Angela Wix at Llewellyn, who is always there for me, giving me encouragement and kind and supportive answers to all my many questions. I'd also like to acknowledge Andrea Neff and Kelly Van Sant, who have been terrific to work with, as well as all the other wonderfully talented people at Llewellyn.

And a heart full of thanks goes to my father, Ronald E. Leland, aeronautical and space engineer, who always believed in my writing, and bought me my first typewriter (it was pink!) to help me with my goal of someday becoming a published author.

DISCLAIMER

Please note that the material within this book is in no way intended to be a substitute for medical or psychological counseling.

$\mathscr{F}$OREWORD
by
DENNIS WILLIAM HAUCK

I first met Dr. Nanci Shanderá in January 2000 at the Lifeways Expo in Pasadena, California. I was lecturing on the application of the operations of alchemy to personal development and modern psychology. Nanci was deeply interested in the alchemical processes I described, and we agreed to meet for breakfast at my hotel the next morning to discuss alchemy further.

I had a great deal of respect for Nanci from the moment I met her. She is an intense, intelligent woman with a refreshingly honest and direct demeanor. When you are in her presence, you know she is fully present and involved in what is going on. You can tell her humility is genuine and born of life experiences.

The more we talked about alchemy, the more impressed I became with her intuitive grasp of alchemical operations. I jokingly accused her of being an ancient alchemist in disguise or at least the reincarnation of one. She seemed wise far beyond her years, and although she was an attractive and vibrant woman, I always pictured her in my mind and dreams as a white-haired tribal elder.

That image fit with Nanci's intense desire to learn spiritual alchemy. She was looking for psycho-spiritual tools to bring back to her "tribe" to help heal and empower them. With this book, Nanci shares what she learned and proved in her practice with the whole world.

The spiritual alchemy Nanci practices is concerned with the trans-formation of the soul. It is the oldest tradition of alchemy and goes back 5,000 years to the priests of ancient Egypt. Spiritual alchemy can be defined as a process of self-realization in which the personality is restructured to express the infinite potential of our true being.

The techniques of spiritual alchemy are designed to clear the mind of its dross and allow unobstructed consciousness and pure being to be directly known. This purification and expansion of conscious-ness is the Philosopher's Stone, the alchemist's most powerful tool for turning lead into gold on all levels of body, mind, and soul. (Author's note: I highly recommend that you watch Dennis William Hauck's tour of his alchemy laboratory on YouTube at http://www.youtube. com/watch?v=-wrV3UcMB5U. In this video, he explains the seven stages of alchemy as an alchemist would work with them in his lab. Hauck also includes the transformational connection with alchemy.)

Nanci demonstrated her knowledge of spiritual alchemy in a series of seven articles she wrote for the *Alchemy Journal*, which were very well received. She showed that alchemical processes are merely sym-bols for the inner process of transforming the "lead" within us into our true golden state of being.

Her basic teaching was that by embracing the gold within, and rais-ing our consciousness to that level, we learn of our soul and its pur-pose. That theme is beautifully expanded in the book before you, and the ingenious tools she provides will guide you step by step through the process.

After our first meeting, Nanci invited me to do an all-day alchemy workshop at the EarthSpirit Center. She founded the group in Los Angeles and later moved it from the city to a lovely Sierra foothills property in Nevada City. I accepted her invitation and returned to Los Angeles to speak on ancient methods of transformation, and how we can apply them to our lives in the modern world.

I believe you can judge a teacher by her students, and Nanci's stu-dents were among the most spiritually advanced and aware groups I have ever spoken to. They already knew the techniques of meditation and how to do spiritual work.

More importantly, her students knew how to create a sacred vessel in which the Great Work of alchemy could take place. I would return to that sacred vessel at EarthSpirit Center many times over the next few years to continue our work together, and all of Nanci's students would become my dear friends.

I think Nanci's greatest talent is simply listening, and often when you are talking with her, you become aware of something rare and magical going on. Her pure attention creates a space in which truth is so welcome, it thrives and takes on a life of its own.

She has an amazing ability to not be distracted by all those little things human beings do to exaggerate, pitch something, conceal things, or change the subject. That is what makes Nanci such a terrific therapist. She has a natural talent for listening and focusing on what is true in what you are saying.

Nanci uses so many different modalities in her work that it is hard to give her a title. I have heard her described as a "spiritual renaissance woman," but even that does not do her full justice. Whatever label you try to put on her, Nanci's work as a teacher, spiritual counselor, ordained minister, mystery school leader, shaman, dreamworker, intuitive artist, and alchemist has changed the lives of hundreds of people. Now, in this new book, she will reach thousands more. Prepare yourself for deep insight and lasting transformation at the hands of this gifted healer.

I think over again my small adventures,
My fears,
Those small ones that seemed so big,
For all the vital things
I had to get and to reach.
And yet there is only one great thing,
The only thing…
To live to see the great day that dawns
And the light that fills the world.

~Old Inuit Song

$\mathcal{I}$NTRODUCTION

This book is intended to assist you in transformational processes that you can use to develop greater recall of your true Self and its relationship to Soul consciousness, your purpose in this lifetime, and unconditional self-acceptance, a key element in the transformation of consciousness. These processes can free us from placing conditions on the way in which we'll become healed or enlightened, upon how we expect others to treat us, or how perfect we must be. When we shift from conditionality to unconditionality, we learn to love without expectation and are freed to experience life as it is meant to flow through us.

Our task as Souls experiencing a human existence is to bring to consciousness and expression the pattern from which we were created as unique and individual emanations of the Divine Mystery. Developing a conscious awareness of these patterns and potential assists the Soul in fulfilling its purpose on Earth, and to evolve and grow through its human experiences.

My pattern, for example, was as a highly sensitive, creative person whose task was to define, further develop, and fine-tune that pattern. Through that process my purpose would emerge, bringing it to my human consciousness, and serve to assist others in doing the same. The key was in developing an unconditional acceptance of myself by transforming the ego-bound state of consciousness in which I had lived for most of my life. I wasn't aware when I was young that while

I was working on mastering the craft of writing, collecting books on Spirit and psychology, and researching everything I could get my hands on about ancient spiritual practices, I was laying a foundation for the eventual conscious integration of my purpose in this lifetime.

My growth would be accelerated when I met and began studying with my master teacher, Brugh Joy, MD, a relationship that lasted for over thirty years. He helped me pull all the rejected parts of myself together in a multidimensional design that would eventually reveal my purpose of serving others through teaching and writing. Even if you don't have a teacher to guide you, there are many things you can do yourself to expand your consciousness.

Alchemy is a powerful and effective system consisting of seven basic stages in which consciousness can be transformed in positive and life-affirming ways. It's generally thought of as a process that turns lead to gold. As I learned more, I realized this was a metaphor for inner transformation. I began to sense a core within my physical body that seemed connected to the energy around me as well. I felt it and saw it in my mind's eye as a beautiful hollow core of gold, through which energies moved within me. I couldn't always access this core, however, because there were aspects of myself that weren't authentic. And that became the work I would do in transforming the many blocks to spiritual consciousness within me.

My teacher would often use words like *nigredo, mortificadio,* and *calcinatio,* which felt familiar, so I dug once more into the mysteries of alchemy and discovered these terms describe difficult experiences as we transform consciousness. The ego stands guard and demands that we remain the same—it does not like change! Though I'm not a laboratory, I believe that as we learn the processes and steps in applying spiritual alchemy to our lives, it is very possible to transform all that is like heavy lead within into the lightness of gold, which is our natural state.

Alchemists believe that the ultimate goal in alchemical transformation is to produce what they call the Philosopher's Stone. This is something that is not attained easily, and never by some. In the various processes of seeking the Stone, we have had to fight through and earn it by working all the alchemical processes of transformation, many times over: incinerating the ego's control; redeeming emotion and intuition; discovering discernment and wisdom; opening the heart through balancing the inner masculine and feminine; integrating lower levels of consciousness with the higher through fire and ferment; distilling all the work already done and developed to a pure essence; and surrendering into a new consciousness of wholeness. Every one of these processes requires a sacrifice, generally consisting of old, outdated, and cherished beliefs.

This book serves as a model for applying the principles of this ancient art-science to the process of personal spiritual evolution. Alchemy refers to "First Matter" as that which lies between the Divine creative urge and its manifestation through Spirit and through us as individuals. Just as in a human birth, this process is born of both creation and chaos as partners in manifestation. The metaphysical and alchemical principle that thoughts become things means that we create our own reality—easy or difficult—by our beliefs. This statement doesn't mean that all we have to do is choose to think good thoughts and we'll have a happy life. The problem with this simplification of a very powerful principle is that adversity is an essential requirement in the act of creation. Individual consciousness work reflects the cosmic relationship of chaos and creation, in how evolution requires a catalyst that causes change and growth. Through the use of alchemical principles, the catalysts are what bring us eventually to recognizing and accepting ourselves as the shining light from that Divine principle of First Matter that created us.

The alchemist's furnace accumulates and brings forth First Matter by reducing its physical properties in burning matter such as dung, urine, menstrum, fertilizer, compost, or night dew. In the alchemist's various containers, the energy of First Matter is concentrated and ultimately becomes an altogether different substance. This new matter is what the alchemist uses in the next procedure, and so on from the next to the next, always deflagrating each substance to bring forth its rich, powerful essence. The processes of alchemy involve various acts of burning or boiling substances as they are transformed into more precious elements. In personal alchemy, we are doing what the alchemists do by burning our overused or outdated attitudes, habits that no longer serve us, beliefs that retard our growth, and fears about our worth. For us, this is not a literal burning process, but as we face the ego's control over us, we may feel that parts of us are being torn or burned away. Our emotions may involve the heat of anger, or the ego may try to rebuild stronger defenses against the painful realizations that are emerging from the darkness into the light. And sometimes the light is just as shocking if we don't recognize ourselves as a being of light, shining with the radiance of all Divine creation.

In their laboratory experiments, alchemists attempt to bring forth gold from lead—the greater from the lesser—in their search for the Philosopher's Stone. We do this in our spiritual transformative work by becoming consciously aware of the play of opposites within and how they have formed a basis for beliefs, biases, and behaviors. In both inner and outer worlds, we may be influenced by powerful and limiting ideas about right/wrong, up/down, above/below, masculine/feminine, dark/light, night/day, you/me, them/us, etc. By being willing to face and transform false beliefs, we discover the fears that underlie truth, and this frees us. In the story of Parsival in chapter 7, the key to what he seeks lies in two essential and powerful questions: "What ails thee?" and "How does this serve?" When we can clearly and honestly answer these questions about our challenges, we transform them. Investigating what it is that truly troubles or upsets us may be difficult work, but a true answer frees us to ask the second question in how the challenge serves us. This may be difficult to answer as well since we are so used to believing things are done *to* us rather than *for* us. It requires releasing any beliefs in victimization. By working through all the exercises and suggestions in this book, you can become more ready and willing to work with these two questions.

Though some alchemists worked to make actual physical gold in their laboratories, the spiritual gold—the Philosopher's Stone—was sought by other alchemists. It represented the perfection revealed by the inner mysteries, which can only be attained by going through the seven basic stages—many times over! Each stage must be fully experienced before it can be embodied and the Philosopher's Stone finally gained.

The essential operations in transformational alchemy lift us from concretized belief and behavior, burn off excess ego and inaccurate and imprisoning beliefs, submerge us in the watery depths of authentic emotion until we accept our essential feeling nature, and dismember us until we surrender to our Soul's purpose. This inner work requires courage because it's always easier to remain unaware of our deeper aspects that seem to hover, shadow-like and terrifying, in the recesses of our minds. Many of us tend to believe that personal healing consists of "getting rid of" our problems, but that's like trying to throw them out the door only to watch them fly back in through the window. We can't get rid of any aspect of ourselves, especially the ego. We can only transform it.

In appendix B at the end of this book, you'll find an exercise called "Writing a New Job Description for Your Ego-Protector." It will assist you in consciously transforming the powerful energy of the ego into an aspect of yourself that supports rather than limits you.

In some of my classes, I combine the study of transformational alchemy and the application of art and creative writing in various processes that mirror the laboratory activities of the alchemists. The creative arts help us find our inner gold by literally seeing in the art projects the alchemical processes of dismembering and transforming egoic self-inflation, compensatory behaviors, alienation, limiting beliefs, and inaccurate perceptions of ourselves. The ego leads us to believe that exploring our depths leads to the destruction of our self, when in truth, alchemical work actually *develops and strengthens* the greater Self while redirecting the influence of the ego to become more of an ally instead of an adversary. It awakens us to the light within as we move through the alchemical stages in which we can discover the gold within us. In appendix C, you will find alchemical art-based projects that you can do to enhance your own transformative processes.

Your Inner Gold presents chapters that define the seven basic stages of alchemical transformation, followed by chapters that help you apply the principles in each stage. We'll begin with *Calcination*, in which the ego's defenses are reduced to ashes in the crucible of Spirit. For those just starting a process of inner work, this may be the most difficult stage of all since it involves intensification of feelings the ego had protected us against experiencing. In appendix A, you can do a process called "The Gold Within You," which helps you understand how your ego works to limit you in order to protect you, which was necessary when you were little. The Gold Within You process shows you how, now as an adult, you can work to transform the ego's protections and thus empower your life.

In the second stage, *Dissolution*, watery emotions mix with the ashes from Calcination to offer us a new perception of our feelings as valuable and necessary. This stage transforms rigid, ego-bound beliefs that were burned in the Calcination stage into water, or tears, which flow when we realize the ego has loosened its control, which for some may be disturbing. We may feel lost or insecure without the ego's direction and restrictive rules to follow.

In *Separation*, we dissect various pairs of opposite ego-influenced aspects within us, such as good and bad, generous and selfish, honest and dishonest, etc., in order to become more conscious of them and how they affect us. In this stage we begin to see more clearly what we processed in the first two stages and are more conscious of the light within us.

This opens a space for a new unification, a sacred marriage, within. This fourth stage, *Conjunction,* balances and integrates opposites and helps us open to heart-based consciousness. As in the Separation stage, we meet new pairs of opposites this time, such as masculine and feminine, and discover their unity when the heart, rather than the ego, directs them.

The fifth alchemical stage, *Putrefaction-Fermentation*, like Calcination, throws us again into the fire. Here, fear-based inner material is burned and rotted away to make space for the development of what has been fermenting in consciousness. In laboratory alchemy, this process involves the decomposition of elements that eventually are reabsorbed as something totally new and beneficial. In spiritual alchemy, this process leads us through our darkness so we can discover our life-affirming, effervescent nature. Sometimes in this fifth stage, a very powerful, yet lesser known, operation called *Mortification* occurs when the materials being putrefied seem to have died but actually herald the onset of a new consciousness—one that brings us closer to the shining light within us, and one that is no longer driven by the ego-protector or old fears. But Mortification involves being humbled—humiliated, in some cases. But, as you will learn from my own *mortificadio* experience that I describe in a later chapter, this challenging experience is more than worth what we go through as it transforms us on deep levels of consciousness.

Distillation, the sixth stage of alchemical transformation, is a delicate yet powerful refinement of the work done in the previous stages. Here, the consciousness has been boiled down to its true essence, no longer directed by ego but rather by the Soul. It is an entirely different state of consciousness, made of the golden light within us. Our distilled essence is far more like Spirit than only the physical aspect of being.

The seventh stage of alchemical transformation, *Coagulation*, is where the alchemist may discover the Philosopher's Stone, the spiritual essence that we have been seeking and that is made manifest as a self-realized consciousness. It brings the seeker full circle, back to Divine Essence where it began—it *coagulates* it, but now with full conscious awareness of the mystery of being—which, in alchemical terms, would mean the transformation from lead to gold has been completed. All that we have processed within ourselves in the seven stages have now been solidified into a new, transformed being and an authentic representation of our essence originally created by the Divine Spirit.

Your Inner Gold presents ways to work with dreams, which are essential elements in alchemical transformation, employed for centuries by alchemists to help them gain wisdom and knowledge in their research. Many people discount the importance of dreams, and relegate them to the realm of fantasy. I've worked with dreams since early childhood, so I know their importance—dreams are the voice of the Soul. Dreams emerge from the imaginal realm from which all creation originates.

Each and every dream reveals our true motivations, experiences, and purpose. Dreams unlock doors to the deep, unconscious forces that we would ordinarily ignore and thereby miss the riches within our personal and the collective consciousness. I highly recommend using a journal in which you can record the details of your dreams and refer back to them often to learn in retrospect things dreams have presented but weren't clear at the time. You can use this journal to write down the results of the meditations and exercises you will find in this book as well.

I also recommend writing your dreams in the present tense. Using the present tense—such as "I am walking down the street" rather than "I was walking down the street"—actually brings you back into the dream itself, and will give it more richness and meaning. Being fully present again in the dream as we write and review it helps fill in parts we may have forgotten, assists us in feeling what we felt in the dream, and makes the interpretation of the dream far more realistic than if it were merely an ordinary event.

Your Inner Gold also examines pre-birth Soul agreements and choices that can help us understand the purpose of our life challenges and relationships with difficult people. We can learn to perceive our experiences as gifts that awaken us instead of proof of our unworthiness. By considering Soul agreements with difficult people in our lives, we learn to understand the fears that motivate their actions. This realization allows us to act from compassion for them rather than reactivity and defensiveness. By this shift in our perception, we are freed from believing ourselves to be victims, and this freedom leads us to the manifestation of our true purpose.

The golden key to becoming conscious rather than merely maintaining horizontal growth is the willingness to open our hearts, no matter what it takes or what we may have to sacrifice. We may have to face fearsome tasks as we dig deep into ourselves. But through the use of alchemical tools, we can free ourselves from fear, and the result is that our hearts will open to our very own shining Philosopher's Stone!

CHAPTER 1

CALCINATION

Incinerating the Ego's Control

"Whatever remains below becomes its own worst enemy."
~ALCHEMICAL ARCANUM ONE

The first stage of alchemical transformation, *Calcination,* is a purification by fire, and a challenging and exacting process of realizing how the ego, through control, inflation, or overprotection, can hold us captive in a prison of limitation. Each alchemical stage is based upon an *arcanum,* which refers to things mysterious, secret, or esoteric. It is a sacred principle or law in alchemy that guides the alchemist in creating gold from lead. In spiritual alchemy, it refers to what the transformative aspect within the stage requires of us in working toward and discovering the gold within us. The arcanum for this stage tells us that Calcination is the process that reveals to us what has been hidden within like untended wounds. It tells us how, when ignored, the wounds and traumas of the past continue to bedevil our lives. The process of Calcination heals this by incinerating the ego's control over us. An alchemist would end up with a pile of ashes, which he would use in the next stage. We end up with the *feeling* that parts of us have been burned to ashes—a tough, sometimes shocking, but always freeing experience. The following imagery meditation will prepare you for what Calcination is and can do.

CALCINATION MEDITATION #1

Relax in a favorite chair, perhaps while playing soft music in the background. Close your eyes and watch your breath, slowly breathing in and out until you are very relaxed.

Begin to consider ways in which your ego has controlled or limited you with its influence. Take time to review all that comes to your attention. Now envision a large red castle on a high hill. Study what it looks and feels like. Begin walking up the hill to the castle. Walk over the drawbridge and knock on the entry gate.

A small, hooded being opens the gate and motions silently for you to enter. He points to a large door and indicates you should go through it. As you do so, you find yourself in a large, round room with carvings on the walls but no windows. There is a large fire pit in the center of the floor.

Now recall the aspect of your ego at the beginning of this meditation that seemed to want your attention the most. Suddenly a paper scroll with a feather pen appears on a small table near you. Sit down and write all you can about this aspect of your ego and how it has affected your life. When you are finished, stand up, roll up the scroll, and stand by the fire.

Set a strong intention to burn this ego aspect to ashes so it will help you let go of it and its control over you. When your intention is strongly set, place the scroll in the fire and watch while it burns. How do you feel as you watch it being consumed by the fire and turned into ashes? A key here is that you are not getting *rid* of this ego aspect, but rather you are transforming it into an energy that will empower yourself rather than your ego.

When the scroll is nothing but ashes, scoop them up and put them in your pocket. It's important to keep the energy, not the activity, of this ego aspect.

Now turn and leave the room and the castle, walking back over the drawbridge and back to your starting place. Review the experience, then write it in your journal.

—————————

Each of the stages of alchemical transformation must be experienced more than once. Each time we go through a stage, we have grown to a certain point, but this doesn't mean we're done with it. As we grow, we wind around and around in a spiral of experience. As our spiral grows wider and higher with these experiences, each time we come to an issue we've worked on before, we go through it again, but this time from a more developed, matured, and transformed state of consciousness. And though I've presented the seven basic stages in order, it's not always typical to experience them in order. The most appropriate stage emerges at the right time in our lives for resolving it. Working in each level of transformational alchemy, over and over, eventually completes the level within you, and previously hidden beliefs are integrated as part of your consciousness.

Next, I've included a meditation that can assist you in exploring hidden beliefs about yourself and how they have affected how you feel about yourself, your authenticity with others, and how you have created your life based upon these beliefs.

Who Am I? Meditation

Close your eyes and ask yourself repeatedly: "Who am I?" As you receive responses to the question, consider that the first answer may not come from a deep enough place of self-awareness. So whatever the answer, counteract it with a response such as, "Not me." Here are just a few examples. I suggest you give yourself time to keep going with this—keep asking the questions over and over. The longer you do this meditation, the more insights you'll glean.

Question: Who am I?
Response: A woman.
Your response to the answer: "Looks like me, but it isn't me."

Question: Who am I?
Response: I own a business.
Your response to the answer: "It's what I do, but it's not me."

Question: Who am I?
Response: A humorous person.
Your response to the answer: "I'm more than that."

Question: Who am I?
Response: Someone who loves swimming and tennis and hiking.

Your response to the answer: "Those are options and preferences, but they don't define me."

Question: Who am I?
Response: A worrier.
Your response to the answer: Again, "Not me."

———⟫•⟪———

This meditation stirs the pot, drawing unconscious material to the surface and clearing the way for development of a more mature and balanced perception of your true golden nature. To base beliefs about ourselves on outer appearances, others' judgments, accepted roles, or learned ideas throws us into illusion, limitation, and inauthenticity. The inner life is eternal and consistently renews and reproduces itself in us as a reflection of our original, Divine design. In giving outer beliefs authority over us, we perceive ourselves falsely. By honoring the inner life, we live from its guidance and know ourselves more deeply. The alchemical stage of Calcination helps to bring to the surface all that may seem hidden, but, in fact, affects us daily on many levels. The more we use the fire of Calcination, the more insights we will gain about our old beliefs, attitudes, and inner fears that have held us back from doing and being what we were intended to do and be.

A clash between arrogance and inadequacy was what I believe my Soul chose before I came into this lifetime as my major challenge, because the potency of it would force me to transform and strengthen my consciousness for the purpose of my Soul's evolvement. My Soul planted the very potent seed of my not having been born the boy my father wanted. This rejection-inadequacy pattern within my life challenge was like the first stage in alchemy, Calcination, where my ego battled over and over which of the two distortions would reign in my life. Being the wrong gender tossed me back and forth between believing that I was rejectable, and compensating for that belief by wearing a mask of arrogance and distancing myself from others.

I once had a dream in which I am the sperm racing other sperm to fertilize the egg that would become me, and its voice keeps repeating: "I've got to get there first, I have to be #1." At the same time, as conception is nearing, I can hear my father's thoughts: "I hope it's a boy, I hope it's a boy." This seed of unacceptability initiated a pre-birth belief in inadequacy, dulling my awareness of my divinity and setting up a desperate need for protection from further pain. As I grew, my ego protected me by cloaking my fears in defenses of superiority alternating with painful shyness.

Because of the early influences and my limited interpretations of my parents' behavior and motivations, it would take years before I no longer perceived my parents or others as having harmed me in *any* way. Several years ago, I learned about the concept of pre-birth Soul agreements, and considered that my parents' Souls had agreed to provide compelling lessons that would impel me to grow as a human and discover my inner gold.

I was to learn that all of the ego's protections were substances in my alchemist's crucible, being ground down to help my Soul evolve by learning to face and transform painful human experiences. Often, when in difficult experiences, which felt like I was burning in the fires of transformation, I was unable to see that as I was reduced to ashes, I became stronger. In time, the ego was reduced in the fire to make space for the true shining self to begin to emerge in consciousness.

In childhood, when we need a variety of ways to protect ourselves, particularly if our physical and emotional environment is unsafe, the deep, wise unconscious self "hires" the ego to do the job we are too young or physically unable to do. Certainly this doesn't always save us from physical or mental abuse, inattention from parents, family traumas, or illness, but it creates a way in which we can discover ways to manage it and to survive. For example, the ego may help us develop an attitude of detachment that numbs emotional pain. It may encourage us to "be nice" so that we don't stir any dangerous pots. Or it may help us "shrink" or become "invisible" so that we don't attract the attention that harms us. It may create an obsessive need for achievement, such as becoming the perfect student or, later, the ruthless corporate executive.

As adults, we can discover that what the ego did for us as children was appropriate, but now this operation is outdated. When we realize our defenses are appropriate to our early childhood and adolescence but not to our adulthood, we may be thrown into an existential crisis of a magnitude that shocks our foundation and rips at our cherished beliefs because it means the old ways must give way to a deeper, truer reality. We may feel like our lives are being dismembered, torn to shreds, burned to ashes, as old patterns are being transformed.

In many of us, the ego protects us by over-inflation so that our reactions to what frightens us exhibit as anger, outrage, arrogance, blame, superiority, and fierce control over anything that seems threatening to the status quo of the ego. All of these protective behaviors may have served us in the past, but when they are no longer appropriate, they damage us because they are a misuse of our authentic power. They feel leaden and keep us from expressing the golden aspects of ourselves.

To learn what Calcination is and how it affects you, try the following meditation to help you identify this stage when it occurs in your life. By learning how to do this, you will be able to work with the situation in a way that helps your Soul evolve and assists you in moving into and through the process of Calcination without ending up feeling powerless.

CALCINATION MEDITATION #2

In a relaxed position, eyes closed, perhaps while playing quiet music, imagine a huge bonfire blocking an entrance to a cave. Take a deep breath and walk through the fire, imagining you will not be harmed. Feel the heat, or even parts of you burning, but continue on until you reach the other side of the fire and see the entrance to the cave. Notice a stairway, which you will descend until you see dark alleyways off to the left and right. There are doors in each alleyway. Pause and ask your inner guidance whether or not to explore the alleyways.

If you get a "no," proceed to the back of the cave, where you will notice a pinpoint of light. As you follow it, it becomes a lighted hallway, which leads into a sanctuary. There, you will become aware of a Being of Light, who sits with you. Ask this Being how you can prepare for your future exploration of the alleyways.

If your inner guidance gives you a "yes," sense which alleyway and which door you feel drawn to. Before proceeding, ask for one of your guides or teachers to join you for protection and guidance.

Move down the alleyway and choose a door. Knock on it, and trust that if you are ready to explore what lies within, it will open. If it doesn't, move to another door and proceed in the same way. Whatever you discover in any room may be at first veiled by your ego's protection. Usually, it will try to steer you away from "danger" by presenting worrisome ideas, thoughts, and visions. So, if the doors open for you, it indicates that you are ready to discover what lies within each room that you explore. Whatever you find must be burned to ashes to release the ego's control in your life.

Be cautious of judging the contents and experiences in the various rooms. Judgment colors experience unrealistically and may even prevent it. As you face whatever you find in each room, you may discover that the unknown doesn't hold the monster you expected. Or, if it does, the willingness to face it confirms your intention to be free.

When you feel complete, move back through the cave the same way you came in. Feel yourself back in your body, imagining it as a body of glowing light, and then open your eyes. Record your experiences in your journal.

———⟫◆⟪———

Alchemists have known for centuries what the quantum physicists are now telling us: that energy changes by observation. When physicists observe atomic particles in huge accelerators, they see the atoms' behavior change in ways that are different when observed by humans than when they are observed by computers. In our inner processes, this means we can transform our problems by carefully and consciously witnessing the energy and activity within the behavior or problem.

In my own case, I observed the ego's various behaviors, such as employing arrogance to mask my fears, or trying to convince me of my worthlessness. This was tough work because I had to observe my ego's behavior for a long enough period of time so it would ultimately reveal its underlying defenses and protections. What I eventually learned, and what really surprised me, was that everything I'd always wanted—strength of mind and character, emotional flexibility, and spiritual awareness—was a basis for the activities of the ego, but was used negatively as protection. I realized that the ego was not an enemy; it had been my protector when I needed it as a young person, but as an adult, I could transform its negative application of my strength into my inner gold. (See appendix A for the process that evolved from my work in observing the ego.)

I had a dream several years ago that demonstrates how beneficial, Soul-related material can emerge from what at first we judge to be dark and unacceptable. This dream illustrates the value of integrating these conflicting forces within.

This dream involved several Mafioso, an apt symbol for the darker aspects of the collective unconscious, which is the unconscious mind we all share. The dream helped me understand that what appeared to be dark and dangerous elements represented by the Mafioso were actually all aspects of myself that needed to be identified, understood, and integrated. This didn't mean I was actually just like these men, but rather they represented dark *symbols* within myself that I might ignore if they were not presented in a powerful way. In most every dream, the characters and beings that appear are parts of ourselves.

In the dream, I am aware that I can't deal with all of the thugs at once, yet I sincerely desire to investigate them, so I lock each of them in separate rooms. I know that if I separate them, I can, on my own terms, become aware of which aspects of myself each of them represent. In alchemy, this is the third stage of transformation, *Separation*, where we look at seemingly incompatible aspects in order to discover their true meaning and potential for transmuting inaccurate perceptions.

A young dog, representing my primal, instinctual nature, appears in the scene. The dog calms the men down by introducing simplicity into complexity. The dog also represents loyalty, in this case, an aspect of myself that is loyal to my cause of transforming my life. Later, I go back to check on each of the men, and I am amazed to see that they are *dis-integrating*, separating into fragments. Their flesh is dissolving, then their bones. In the spiritual practice of shamanism, this is called *dismemberment*, a necessary inner process if we are to become authentic and whole, and very similar to Calcination. Dismemberment teaches us that the sacrifice of our belief about ourselves may be the key to becoming whole again.

In my dream, just as in Calcination, the Mafioso are sacrificed by becoming piles of ash. Ash is used by alchemists in combination with other substances to deepen their experiments into the next level of transformative evolution. In my dream, the men's ashes represent what must be burned out within me if I am to become conscious.

As I begin to realize this, the Mafioso's remains rearrange themselves into a single human form. This represents a re-integration of essential parts of myself that I had denied and rejected.

The single Mafioso figure in my dream still appears dark and powerful, but in a way that empowers the new, integrated composition of myself. The darkness has been transformed—not dismissed or rejected—from potential danger to potential creativity. It is that place within us that is sacred, private, and precious. The darkness shields certain creative aspects of ourselves just as we might safeguard our valuables in a bank deposit box—which is dark inside but protects and nurtures our inner riches.

In the final scene of this dream, I am putting on a golden robe by a beautiful altar. Putting on the robe—or mantle—means that I am consciously embracing the rejected or denied aspects of myself as necessary elements of wholeness.

When working with dream imagery and symbol, the key is to *integrate* both mental-analytical and emotional-intuitive elements brought forth by the dream. By honoring the mental, cognitive, reasoning side of us, we quiet the ego's need to control. The ego is at home in the intellectual realm and therefore has little need to disguise and defend against revelation of the dream's true meaning. It revels in exploring words, phrases, and ideas. The emotional-intuitive side of us is at home in the actual dream itself, with its symbols, sometimes obscure or esoteric, and its creative ways of presenting issues and inspirations.

Dreams hold a particular value in how they demonstrate to us our beliefs and how they influence us in all aspects of our lives. When we have dreams about our beliefs, we can work with them to discover how firmly entrenched they are and how they affect our perceptions of life. The following exercise will help you discover beliefs that affect your life through how you perceive yourself. This is particularly helpful in discovering how often we say, think, or feel negative things about ourselves.

Belief Awareness Exercise

Write a list of the problems and challenges in your life in your journal, such as, "I am unhappy," "I am unloved/unlovable," "My children hate me," "I won't ever be good enough," "I have no talents or skills," "I am always ill," "I'll probably die young," "I can't succeed because I was abused as a child," etc.

Make this list as long as possible, perhaps taking a few days to complete it. Make sure you've covered everything that bothers you about yourself.

When your list feels complete, go back and add "I believe" before each item.

Your list will look something like this: "*I believe* I am unhappy," "*I believe* I am unloved/unlovable," "*I believe* my children hate me," etc.

Now look at each item and explore how it feels and what it seems to be showing you now that you've shifted your perception of the issue. Do you feel a difference between merely stating what you think of as a *fact* and looking at it as a revealing statement that is based upon a *belief* and not actually fact after all? You might question where you got the belief in the first place. Was it influenced by parents, teachers, friends, lovers, or society? If you can identify its source, it will be easier to transform.

I encourage you to continue to explore *facts* as you have always seen them, then bring yourself up to date by changing your perception of them as beliefs that you can change. As you continue doing this exercise, old, deeply submerged perceptions of yourself may emerge. You may be surprised by what you discover.

By transforming attitudes toward adversity from an affliction to a gift that can move you closer to your inner gold, you *redeem* frozen emotions from events of the past. By working in this way, you cease *reactivating* those events and recharging the fear-filled beliefs and feelings that have been held within them. The following exercise is related to the previous one, but it takes you even deeper into realizations about how your beliefs create your experience. In this exercise, you'll learn to become more aware of how this occurs and what you can do about it.

Clearing the Past Exercise

To learn how you might be unconsciously reactivating events of the past, think about a time when you were involved in a really prickly problem and began talking about it, over and over, to whoever would listen.

Did the incessant talking help you heal the situation? Why not? Observe how you kept reactivating it each time you told the story.

The energy you put into it was not one of desire for authentic resolution, but rather your ego's way of protecting you from diving into the difficult work of transformation by maintaining a belief in victimization. By continually resurrecting the issue and putting energy into it, our belief in it as a fact increases.

Now imagine creating a different reality by thinking again about the same problem. See and feel yourself finding another way to resolve it by not talking about it to others. Imagine yourself sitting with the problem as if your issue were a person. Dialogue with it, asking it what it has to teach you and how you can be more aware of how to work with it in the future. By dialoguing with the actual problem itself, you will learn its underlying meaning and purpose. For example, there may be a person in your life who gives you a hard time. Rather than complaining about her to friends, take yourself to a place you like—maybe your meditation corners or a garden. Imagine the difficult person sitting across from you, both of you in agreement to explore without criticism or attack. Ask this person why she treats you as she does, what her feelings are toward you, how she feels about herself when she criticizes you, etc. The most important task for you is to listen—deeply—to what she has to say. If your intention is clear enough, you won't be tempted to manufacture what you think she'd say, so you can justify your hurt feelings. Do this exercise with an open heart. This is the way to receive the authentic answers you want and need.

When you are done, write everything down in your journal and watch what happens next time you're with this person. A miracle may not happen at once, but if you keep what you learned in mind, things will change between you. You will receive and grow so much more than when you were just gossiping about her with your friends, who were probably tired of hearing the same complaints!

————⟫◆⟪————

I've always loved Charles Dickens' classic *A Christmas Carol*, because it illustrates how we entrench ourselves in pain and defenses because of our fear-based beliefs. Resolution is impossible until someone demands that we change, as happened with the appearance of the spirits who visited Ebenezer Scrooge. As the old curmudgeon reviews his life, he is able to see where he *missed the mark* (in archery, the word for this is "sin") and rejected the love within himself and from others. In the end, thanks to the journey guided by the spirits, he decides to open his heart and become a beloved member of his community. Opening our hearts and changing our perceptions is the inner work of alchemical transformation.

True transformational work requires that we consider what most might consider wrong or unacceptable in order to discover what lies underneath. When we are born into the denser energies of physical, earthly life, and our Soul's purpose fades from our memory, we begin a journey of challenge until we are willing to surrender to the path of introspection that our Souls wish us to travel. It seems kind of crazy, doesn't it, to be free within a clear sea of spirit, and then to actually *choose* to drop down into a human experience in order to endure what we must if we are to learn life's lessons. We experience the physical pain of being born, the emotional pain of knowing deep down that we cannot, at least temporarily, access the unutterable realm from which we came, and the mental pain of knowing we can't do anything about it until we learn what earthly life has to teach us. Then, and only then, can we remember who we truly are and from where we originate, discovering that it is not independent of earthly experience, but is an expansive, inclusive realm of unified consciousness.

An important key in transformation is not to reject things about ourselves, but to unearth the deeper meaning in whatever appears to be rejectable. It is the action of the spiritual alchemist not to throw something out, but to learn how to include it in the process, which then gains power and leads to greater awareness. To be fully self-accepting means being completely unconditional with yourself, no matter what you are doing, thinking, or feeling. The dictionary defines *unconditionality* as "without conditions or reservations; absolute," and *absolute* as "pure and simple, unadulterated, undiluted, complete, authentic, and genuine." How do you feel when you perceive those words as describing yourself? How does your heart respond? Do you feel a sense of freedom? Or do you feel sad, believing you can never match up to these virtues? Try looking in a mirror in the middle of an embarrassing or devastating moment, then smile at your image and say, "Hey, kid. You're okay, just the way you are." This is you being unconditional with yourself, not judging or rejecting. If you can't smile, at least don't judge yourself—this is another way you are accepting yourself unconditionally in that moment.

By changing how you've always perceived adversity—as well as how you imagined you've been perceived by others—you can discover what's *right* with you. This is not "positive thinking" in the way many think of it as denial, covering up, or rejection of uncomfortable or unacceptable experience and replacing it with "nice." When we seek only the acceptable, we guarantee ourselves disappointment and disillusionment. When we *welcome* adversity and discomfort as powerfully effective teachers, we move closer to self-realization. *All* experience is important and essential, no matter how difficult. Think of the alchemist in the laboratory, adding chemicals and other substances to his beakers and retorts. The potent mixtures bubble away, creating all kinds of strange sounds and strong aromas. When something doesn't seem to work, the alchemist doesn't toss it in the garbage. Instead, he considers how it might be teaching him something that he needs to know about his next alchemical process, how this may lead to inspired breakthroughs. He knows that by approaching problems in this way, he will eventually reach the gold he seeks.

Just like the alchemist who doesn't throw away unpleasant substances he's using, we can choose to face our discomfort rather than ignoring or rejecting it. When we find our core of strength that helps us accept *all* parts of ourselves, *unconditionally*, we become more authentic. I believe we are all "multiple personalities," not in the medical-pathological sense, but in how we are composed of many different aspects of self. Accepting our many aspects, without judgment, is a key to transforming our limitations.

If you are interested in observing some of your multiple aspects, here's a visualization exercise that can show you clearly how aspects of yourself behave and interact with each other. It employs the witness or observer part of ourselves that was mentioned earlier as a tool of alchemists and quantum physicists.

Multiple Aspects Exercise

Relax in your favorite posture, close your eyes, and imagine yourself in a theater, sitting in the back row. Open your consciousness to your Inner Observer aspect, which watches without judgment of any kind—it merely observes. Your Observer is aware of another part of yourself standing on the stage, lit by a spotlight. We'll call this your Personality aspect. As the spotlight illuminates the Personality, the Observer also sees a dark silhouette appear. This is your Shadow self.

Watch the Personality as it acts onstage—walking, dancing, bending, looking around, or talking. Observe the Shadow and what it is doing. Pay particular attention to how it might be affecting the Personality. What does the Shadow do that the Personality may not be aware of? How does the Personality act as a result of not knowing what the Shadow is doing? What happens if the Shadow approaches and tries to interact with the Personality? How does the Personality react to that? Does the Personality turn away? Does it collapse in fear? Does it do battle with the Shadow? What happens if it discovers a way to interact or converse with the Shadow in an attempt to learn its purpose? Allow enough time to fully experience the whole play between the Shadow and Personality.

In the final scene, your Observer sees a bright light, brighter than the stage lights. This light moves toward the Personality and the Shadow, surrounding and embracing them until they are immersed in it. This light is your Soul Self, your inner gold. Be aware of how this feels to have these three aspects of self integrated.

Now blend your Observer with the light of your Soul. What do you see? What do you feel? What do you sense about the Personality and the Shadow?

Complete your meditation by honoring all these aspects of yourself, and feel your connection to them. Sit for a while with this feeling, then open your eyes and record your experience in your journal.

The Observer self helps us learn from our various aspects instead of running away from what appears to be unacceptable by our limited—and learned—standards. By transforming our perceptions, the "rejectable" parts of ourselves become allies in strength, courage, and authenticity. We do this by reconsidering *everything* we've been taught about what's "nice" or acceptable. (I advocate "nice-ectomies"!) To be a true alchemist of your life, step out of the acceptable and the "normal," and try doing what you've always dreamed of doing!

⟹⬧⟸

In the next chapter, we'll explore how we can work with dreams as alchemical tools that can deepen our understanding of our experiences and purpose on Earth. Every dream we have fits in one or more of the alchemical stages, and as we learn how to interpret what they are telling us, we are strengthened as we experience the various stages. Dreams often seem impossible to interpret, but you can learn how to identify your own personal dream symbology as clues that make interpretation much easier, especially when you look at the symbols from an alchemical viewpoint. Learning how to understand dreams is an important gift that you can apply to every part of your life.

Summary Points

- Calcination is a transformation by fire of the ego's control over us.
- Calcination's alchemical arcanum tells us that anything unexplored within us becomes one of our challenges.
- Each alchemical stage must be experienced more than once.
- Our beliefs, attitudes, and habits are influenced by the ego.

- Calcination's fire may be painful but necessary to loosen the ego's control.

- The ego's original job is to protect us while young; as adults, the protections are no longer helpful or appropriate.

- Transformation requires objective, unconditional observation.

- Changing perceptions from "fact" to "belief" shows us what holds us back from being our authentic, golden selves.

- Transforming belief in adversity helps us redeem repressed and important emotions.

- Transformation requires exploring aspects of self that may seem unacceptable.

- Rejection versus self-acceptance is an important key to transformation.

CHAPTER 2

DREAMS

*How They Guide Us
Through Transformation*

One of the more potent ways we can deepen our experience with Calcination and all levels of alchemy is through dream work. This is essential in personal spiritual transformation and connects with alchemical experiences because both originate from the deep self and lead to awakening of consciousness. Both dreams and alchemical processes assist us in resolving important issues, becoming aware of strengths and weaknesses, healing the body, inspiring creativity, understanding our past, opening us to a greater spectrum of feelings, and ultimately taking us to higher realms of consciousness. The relationship between the alchemical stages and dreams is mutually beneficial because each contribute to a deeper wisdom and fuller experience of life. Basically, dreams give us pictures of what we are transforming, and can present wisdom and insight that guide us through whatever stage we are working with.

Since I will be presenting dreams throughout this book, I encourage you to use the journal mentioned in the introductory chapter to record your dreams and experiences. I also recommend that you write your dreams in the present tense rather than past tense: "I am walking down the street" rather than "I walked down the street." This helps you move back into the dream, which reveals its richness and meaning. Being present once again in our dreams helps to fill in the blanks, assists us in feeling what we were feeling while dreaming, and provides a more accurate interpretation because we are once again an active part of the dream. Additionally, you can stimulate dreaming by repeating strong statements before you fall asleep: "I want to have a dream. And I want to remember it." This may not happen immediately, but if you keep programming your subconscious to release the dreams to your memory, you'll eventually be able to remember and record them when you wake. I recommend you date each one. It's also a good idea to give each dream a theme title—this helps to connect similar dreams that you can work on as a life theme.

In 1982 I had a powerful, transformational dream that I call a Life Dream because it describes the various levels of growth we can encounter during a lifetime. This dream kept coming back to my awareness for years, so I kept working on its message. As time went by, my interpretations changed as I grew. And as I began to study alchemy, I realized that the dream included many of the seven stages of alchemical transformation, such as Calcination, which would gradually help me to incinerate thoughts and beliefs I'd been carrying that deceived me in thinking I was far less than I was. The dream also involved Dissolution and Distillation, whose watery aspects are related to dreaming and emerge from deep within our liquid subconscious, where symbols and emotions ebb and flow.

This dream is set in ancient Egypt. I am walking with others down into an Olympic-size pool, seven feet in depth. This represents my descent into the subconscious as well as the seven stages of alchemy. All of us in the pool look like various Egyptian gods—very tall, half-human, half-animal. My head is birdlike, with a long beak, representing Thoth, the god of writing who communicates the messages of the gods to humanity. We stand equidistant from one another, completely submerged in the pool, and able to breathe easily underwater.

At the end of the pool is a small orchestra pit where an extremely tall being stands. I recognize him as Khnum, the god of creativity who brings the life force into humanity. He is a master alchemist in what he does for us as initiates. Khnum reaches down into a pit containing ancient stoneware bowls—like the crucibles that are used by alchemists to mix various substances—and he begins tossing each one like a discus toward each of us. He throws three my way, and I am surprised and delighted that I can catch them effortlessly. They are small, plainly decorated bowls and I stack them one inside another, tucking them under my right arm. These three bowls represent the first three stages of transformational alchemy, which are foundational for the higher alchemical stages.

So I begin to long for one of the large bowls, because they are the most beautiful. At the moment I feel this desire, Khnum throws me a sizable one, shaped like a serving bowl. I'm afraid I won't be able to catch it while holding the smaller ones, but I catch it neatly and feel relieved and thrilled as the dream ends.

It took me years to learn that the dream symbolized the Soul agreement I had made before this lifetime to be of service to humanity—thus, the *serving* bowl. But it was going to require a tremendous amount of work throughout my life to build the inner strength necessary to fully embody this assignment. It would require repeated journeys in and through each alchemical stage until I finally reached Coagulation, which represents service to humanity.

At first, the work was arduous due to difficult self-esteem issues colliding with what I always sensed I was here to do—I experienced Calcination and the other first stages many times over until the influence of the ego had lessened. Besides representing the first three alchemical levels, I eventually recognized the three smaller bowls as *planter* pots, depicting the first three stages of my life—childhood, adolescence, and young adulthood—when I would sow the seeds of growth in preparation for the fourth and final stage of my current lifetime. The fourth bowl, a *serving* bowl, was a symbol for my work in service through writing and communicating the inner mysteries in my classes and writing. It formed the container for my experiences in the alchemical Distillation and Coagulation stages.

To discern if you have had a Life Dream, look back at major dreams you've had, ones you couldn't seem to interpret but that have followed you for years. Usually, Life Dreams will be vividly colored and present a mystical theme because they come directly from our higher selves, our Soul and Spirit. I suggest you research the symbols in your dream, or certain words that continue to hold your attention. Look them up in a thesaurus for related words that may give you clues as to the direction the dream wants to take you. Life Dreams are not meant to solve problems on the human level, so don't look for that. Look instead for metaphors in them that speak to you about who you are and why you are here. Look at the dream piece by piece through meditations. Ask the dream to reveal its meaning to you. If you keep working on it, it will reveal your inner gold!

We also have dreams that reveal life patterns and challenges from the past, present, or even future. I had a dream when I was seven that was partly a Calcination dream because it involved intense heat (my mother's birth pains) in a crucible (my mother's uterus, from which I was emerging). The dream is vividly colored (an indication that it was presented from a higher part of my consciousness), and there are green drapes on either side of me. In front of my line of sight is a table covered with more green fabric. On the table are what look to me to be brightly colored celluloid toothpicks. An angry, frowning face appears. It is a woman with curly blond hair, who keeps repeating sharply, "Don't touch that! Don't touch that!" To my seven-year-old dreaming mind, this was terrifying because I thought she was yelling at *me*. Years later, I discovered the dream was a recall from my birthing experience as I emerged from the canal—I can see the green sanitary drapes over my mother's legs, but I can also see the process from above and am able to see everyone in the delivery room. I recognize the yelling woman as a nurse, telling my mother, not me, to stop trying to pull the drapery aside so she can see me. My mother, in her twilight sleep daze, really wants to reach for me, but it wasn't allowed in those days. The table covered with the green fabric is what the doctors were using, and what looked like colored toothpicks to my young mind are actually the silver instruments on the table, glittering in the lights.

Because of the trauma of the birthing process added to the nurse's negative bullying, I am born believing that my mother doesn't want to touch me and is the one doing the yelling—I was confusing her with the nurse. This, along with my father's wish for a boy, set the stage for my struggle with rejection that, combined with all my other life challenges, would eventually lead me back to my true Self through the hard work of remembering that I indeed had been wanted and loved by my parents in their own way. But the process of finally remembering took many *Calcination* experiences throughout my life—ones that would take me back to the fire of rejection until I finally understood what had actually occurred. The alchemical arcanum for Calcination, "Whatever remains below becomes its own worst enemy," was true for me during most of my life until I was able to bring the pain of rejection to the surface of my consciousness and work to heal it.

Dreams originate in the deep, expanded realms of our consciousness. Since this is so foreign to many of us, what we remember of our dreams are snippets, edited by our egos, which lead us to doubt the value of our dreams. When we dismiss the very real importance of dream symbology and messages, we sacrifice valuable information that we need to be whole. We downplay this important part of life in order to be accepted as "normal." In the 2008 ABC television series *Eli Stone*, the main character is avoiding his spiritual calling and longs to be "normal." A deity figure, played by Sigourney Weaver, tells Eli that *normal* is just another word for *sloth*, which, she says, is a failure of potential.

Dreams teach us that our own personal symbology is related to archetypal, or universal, symbology. A book on symbology and archetypes is more helpful than books that propose to interpret dream symbols because all they do is offer the same meaning for all. I recommend combining universal symbology with what you gather as personal symbols in order to understand your dreams and their messages. You can also apply this symbology to your everyday life, because there is actually no difference between dream reality and ordinary reality—they are merely extensions of one another in different forms. Many times we'll dream about something that happened that day, but the dream scenario looks so different from the daytime reality that we miss the connection. If we fail to make the connection, we may lose the wisdom the dream is offering us about the daytime experience.

Using this combined approach will build your confidence in your ability to interpret your life experiences in the same way as you do your dreams. You'll learn that common dream symbols, like fire or water, for instance, usually refer to emotions, change, resistance, or the flow of energy or lack of it. An example might be in a dream you have of being swept away in a raging river. Generally, water represents emotion, change, or spirit, so for you it might symbolize the loss of something that you've held dear, whether it's a person, job, or way of thinking and being, and how you feel about that loss or change.

Your river dream would be a Dissolution dream because it involves water that you cannot control and that takes you to another place in consciousness. Another example is a dream in which something of importance to you is being destroyed by fire, as in Calcination, which burns away that which we ignore or refuse to deal with and that may present as ongoing anger. In a Calcination dream, the fire burns and you are given the opportunity in the dream to resolve the chronic anger by looking at what the burning object means to you symbolically. It could be that your apartment is on fire and could possibly mean that you really don't want to be living there and haven't taken any steps to remedy the problem—thus the fire represents your anger at yourself and your indecision.

ALCHEMICAL THEMES IN DREAMS

Here is a brief list of some of the themes that may appear in alchemical dreams. Keep in mind that some of these may apply to more than one level of alchemical dreaming. You may not see these exact actions in your dreams, but you may be able to connect various events in the dreams to some of the things on this list, making it easier for you to begin to recognize what the dream is telling you from a transformational alchemical standpoint.

To apply anything on this list to a dream event, find a word or phrase on the list that you sense has the same or a similar theme to what happened in the dream. (You can use your thesaurus here.) Check which alchemical stage the theme appears in (it might be in more than one stage), and you'll know where to focus your attention in terms of what the dream is telling you. An example would be that you've just dreamed that your boss yelled at you in front of all the other employees. You'd find the corresponding alchemical theme in the first and last items under *Calcination*. You'll know from this that the work your Soul wants you to do is in transforming the ego-controller—the boss plays this role in the dream—and surrendering to your authentic self.

Calcination

- A raging fire offers the greatest potential for change
- Reduction to ash
- Burning out of ego attachments to "things," beliefs, defenses
- Humbling or humiliation, surrender

Dissolution

- Dissolving that which was burned out in Calcination by water (tears, crying, emotion)
- Immersion into the unconscious, formless, feminine
- Conscious surfacing of old material
- Waters washing away unneeded material

Separation

- Jumping, being pushed, or falling off a precipice
- Dismemberment, feeling you or your life is falling apart
- A deeper review of material discovered in Dissolution
- Beginning to consciously accept and reintegrate previously rejected strengths and gifts
- Sorting out shame, guilt, or beliefs that no longer serve
- Transforming blocks to the Soul's purpose and gifts
- Learning what your deepest fears or sufferings are

Conjunction

- Engagement of the masculine and feminine forces
- Bringing opposites together in new ways that may have been discovered in Separation
- Deepening of intuitive awareness
- Clarity of mind and purpose
- Clarity of the relationship between inner and outer, Earth and Heaven: as above, so below

Putrefaction-Fermentation

- Cycle of being immersed in the lower energies, then arising in the higher
- Facing the unthinkable as you become aware that it is being transformed into what you need
- Birth of a new life being born in you
- Strengthening the new life through acceptance and embodiment of the shadow

Distillation

- Desire to deepen the inner process through meditation and prayer
- Embodying the spirit of the transformational process
- Condensing results of Fermentation into pure essence
- Integration of inner forces to transform ego inflation
- Integrating wisdom
- Transforming lower-level emotions
- Transforming identity from ego to authenticity

Coagulation

- Knowing the feeling of *being* with the Presence of Spirit
- Further purification of Distillation
- New experience of self that transcends the past or need for a future
- Communion with the Soul
- The ultimate, perfect healer of all imbalance and disharmony
- Transcendence of all previous beliefs
- The Philosopher's Stone... the gold within you

Working with dreams is not actually a process of interpreting the dreams, but rather of interpreting ourselves. I believe this is why most people won't work with their dreams, because the prospect of perceiving one's deep mysteries clearly and completely can seem frightening or unimportant. This is particularly difficult if we reject the concept that, to become whole, we must embody what lies in shadow as well as in light. There is a vast difference between the darkness I refer to and the misuse of it, which we call "evil." Our problem with the dark lies within our deep, learned fears about it, which are subjective and personal, as well as collective. But have you noticed that many times whatever you fear never manifests? Darkness itself, that hidden, shadowy world within us, is not "evil" at all when experienced as a place within us that holds our power—and it's up to us as to how we use it. Transformation of fear into power is accomplished by accepting both light and dark forces within us without being blocked by judgment.

In two dreams of Calcination and Fermentation I had several years ago, they threw me into the fire of my deep fears about myself. Recurring dreams with the same theme, even if presented in different scenarios, occur when there is an important issue we've been ignoring. These dreams happen again and again until we are willing to accept the message within them and make the appropriate course corrections.

In the first dream, my younger daughter and I are lying on our stomachs on a brick hearth, looking at a fireplace several feet away. Suddenly, out of the fireplace emerges the huge monster from the film *Poltergeist*. At first, we are shocked, but we become fascinated as a stack of beautifully wrapped gifts appear in front of the beast, who slowly begins pushing the gifts toward us. The creature withdraws into the fireplace and just waits, watching.

The monster, a symbol for the fear within me that I didn't yet understand, appeared from the *hearth*, a word referring to the heart of a home, or symbolically, in this case, as my true self. The fireplace was an alchemical reminder that illustrated the burning out of my ego-based beliefs and behaviors in order to eventually find the gold within me.

In the dream, my daughter and I question whether or not we should open the gifts, but they begin opening themselves. The wrappings and ribbons fall away as the box lids pop open. We cautiously look inside the boxes and are awestruck at what lies within: a variety of beautiful crystal figurines of deities and angels. The gifts are symbolic of the shining light within me that I had not yet recognized. But the most important gift in the dream was the appearance of the monster, who personified a fearsome, negative part of myself that compensated for my low self-esteem.

In the second dream, I am touring a lighthouse—again, a symbol for the light within me—and begin ascending (moving into higher consciousness in the Fermentation stage) a circular stairway inside it to the top of the structure. When I am about halfway up, the *Poltergeist* monster, once again, appears in front of me, this time in a far more threatening manner than in the previous dream. I am terrified when it points its long, bony finger at me and says in a deep, resonant voice, "I am *you*!" In Fermention, a catalyst is always required for change to occur. In this dream, the monster was that catalyst, showing itself the second time to stir the alchemical substance within the process I was in so I could eventually become distilled and own the power that the monster had held for me for so long.

These two dreams revealed my fears that had been preventing me from realizing the power within me that I could use to good purpose. It had to present itself to me as a monster to demonstrate my belief that I had no power, even though I had been unconsciously misusing power in my arrogant behavior. When I dealt with the shocking feelings in these two dreams, I was able to see how I had indeed been the monster in many of my interactions with people, in my work, and in my inner relationship with myself. But I also saw that what I had created as a monster was my naive understanding of power, which I thought was bad until I learned that it was actually not a monster at all but rather a very strong aspect of my authentic self. I had been so used to using power over people that I didn't know it was a positive element of my being that I'd been misusing.

Dream Characters as Parts
of Ourselves Exercise

Working with each character in our dreams as parts of ourselves is an important key to accurate interpretation. Here
are some questions you can ask as you review each person or
character—or even an object that draws your attention in your
dream:

- Why has this character, person, or object appeared in my dream?

- What is it about this person or character that is similar to myself?
  (Even if a person in a dream is someone you know in ordinary
  reality, in most cases it is not the actual person, but rather an
  aspect of yourself that the person represents to you.)

- What is this character trying to tell me about myself or something in my life by its actions?

- If a character in a dream appears as a monster figure, what does
  it tell you about yourself? What does it tell you if it appears as a
  dainty fairy princess? Or a strong, handsome prince?

- If you could ask each character one question, what would it be?
  And what do you learn from its answer?

- How is this character serving your growth process?

———◆———

I believe that as we develop dream methodology, we learn that we
can apply the same processes to situations in our waking lives. There
is really no difference, in my experience, between any realities, dream
or ordinary, but only in how we perceive them. The following is an
example of this.

In 1996, I led a tour to several sacred sites in Britain. We visited
Stonehenge, Avebury, Merlin's Cave, and a variety of stone circles, all of
which were certainly magical and mysterious. One of the women had
been working on releasing an abusive man from her life for some time
with no success. She felt it was because there was such a strong energetic connection between them that she couldn't let go. One night while

we were in Avebury, she had a nightmare that the man was threatening her with a sword.

The next morning when we did our daily dream processing, she was clearly very shaken by the dream. I suggested she find some kind of physical representation of the sword and do something, like break it, which would symbolize severing their connection. She mulled the idea over for a few days, and then, when we arrived in Glastonbury, she found "the sword," which was a tree branch, lying in the middle of her path. It was the same size and shape as the man's sword in her dream, but because it was green, she couldn't break it. She listened to her inner guidance and saw a leather sheath in her mind's eye. When she opened her eyes, there was a hole in the hedgerow exactly the right size for the sword. As she shoved the sword-branch into the opening, thereby sheathing it, she felt the energy shift between her and the man, and knew she had finally and successfully disconnected from him. Though there was no fire in her dream or her ritual, this experience was related to the way that Calcination requires a battle, with either fire or sword, with the ego's hold on the way we remain stuck in situations from our past. In her case, her sword freed her from the abuse of the past. It was also a Conjunction dream in how it helped her use both her feminine and masculine aspects to resolve it.

Different dreams come from different levels of consciousness within us. We may have a dream in which our physical body tells us something about it that we need to know. This may not present itself in a simple, literal way because of the symbolic language of dreams. Consequently, a dream about your body may appear as a broken-down building in a shabby neighborhood, which would be a warning to take better care of yourself or that something in your body is breaking down and should be checked out.

The illustration in figure 1 represents the energy bodies that emanate from us and surround our physical bodies. Our dreams can originate in any of these realms of consciousness. The more spiritually oriented levels are less dense than the physical, so when we dream, meditate, go out of body, or have a visionary experience or sudden, clear realization, our consciousness is in one of these higher, more expanded levels. This is why it may be difficult to remember or inter-pret these higher dreams and experiences. As we begin the re-entry process in waking, we generally don't bring back all that was experi-enced because it originated in another layer of our energy fields. If a dream emanates from the spiritual realm of consciousness, the mean-ing may seem so obscure that by the time it filters down to the physi-cal, as we stretch and move about upon waking, the dream is lost or even misread as something far less potent.

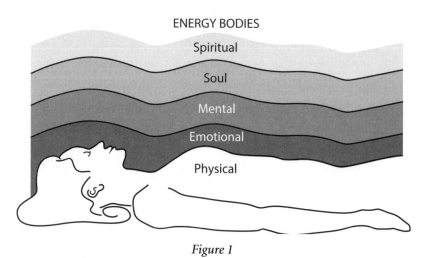

Figure 1

I recommend keeping your dream journal or a simple pad of paper with pen or pencil nearby at night. This way you can easily reach over, even in the dark, jot down a few key words from your dream, and go back to sleep. Then, as you begin to wake in the morning, hold your body still. Moving disturbs the memory of the dream that is actu-ally held in the cells. After mentally reviewing it, you can then sit up and write the details of the dream. Some people like to decorate their journals, since the subconscious will give us more dreams if it knows we honor them by keeping them in a sacred place. Putting dreams on little scraps of paper that get lost impresses upon the subconscious the idea that dreams are not really important, so it won't offer up as much as when you respect this valuable aspect of your life.

This is why I've kept dream journals all of my life. I can go back and review my dreams from years past and get their wisdom and guidance at any time. My journals are actually large three-ring binders filled with dreams I've recorded on a typewriter or computer and then hole-punched to fit in the binder. I make periodic marginal notes on what I sense the dream is telling me. When I go back to the dream, sometimes years later, I'll rework it and add new notes. This shows me how much I've grown over the years and many times reveals an answer to a question that my life at the time of the dream didn't have. I recommend going back through your dream journals every six months and reading the dreams of that period to review and learn from them.

The most often asked question about dreams is how to remember them. The task is simple but requires consistency. By keeping your pad and pen by your bed, and setting a strong intention every time you go to sleep that you want to have a dream and remember it, you will begin to recall your dreams. This may take time, so don't quit—keep trying.

Beginning to work with dreams is like standing on one side of a beautiful river, longing to know what's on the other side but not yet having a way to get across. As we work more with our dreams, we learn to stand with one foot on each bank, steady in the knowledge that both sides, including the river itself, are an integral part of our spiritual evolvement. When we work with our dreams in this way, we become a bridge that gives us access to all realities.

The alchemical arcanum for the first level of transformational alchemy, Calcination, "Whatever remains below becomes its own worst enemy," aptly describes what happens if we ignore our dreams. When we have dreams that involve fire, burning, or frenzied activity, even though they may be frightening, the dreams bring up issues that we have ignored. And when we are consciously aware of the issues, we can do something about them. They no longer have to fester within us, affecting aspects of our lives that could otherwise be creative and flowing with the golden energy of our true selves.

In the next chapter on the second process of personal alchemy, *Dissolution,* we will learn how the element of water affects us by dissolving hardened parts of our ego-based emotions. What has been burned in

Calcination is mixed with water in Dissolution, forming a new way of dealing with the ego through more conscious recognition of the value of our feelings.

Summary Points

- Working with dreams is a powerful way to work with Calcination and all other levels of alchemical transformation—they all originate from the deep self.

- Dreams picture what we are going through in our alchemical processes and present the wisdom and insights we need to assist the process.

- Always record your dreams in the present tense, since this brings the dream back in a fuller and more meaningful way.

- Pre-sleep programming to remember dreams and keeping a journal by your bed help to bring forth more dreams with more details.

- Identifying your own Life Dream can empower you and lead you to discover your Soul's purpose while on Earth.

- Life-pattern dreams can show us the roots of our ongoing challenges.

- There is great value in learning your own dream symbology.

- We're not just interpreting our dreams—we're interpreting ourselves.

- Darkness in dreams is not "evil"; these dreams teach us how to balance dark and light, which assists us in our wholeness.

- Fear-based dreams containing dark characters teach us about parts of ourselves that we have ignored or feared.

- When we ignore our dreams, whatever they are trying to tell us will become our problems.

CHAPTER 3

DISSOLUTION

Freeing Emotion and Intuition

"The way to truth is through Intelligence of the Heart."
~ALCHEMICAL ARCANUM TWO

The second stage in transformational alchemy, *Dissolution*, is the process that reveals how our emotions are influenced by the ego and how we can redeem them and use them appropriately. As you work with Dissolution, emotions may break open as a way to learn about them. Alchemists value tears because they contain one of the three main elements—salt—used in the alchemists' laboratory. (The other two elements are sulphur and mercury.) By adding the water of our tears to the ashes of incinerated beliefs in Calcination, Dissolution helps us to feel and understand our emotions more clearly. Conscious crying or other expression of emotion can help to release old beliefs of past experiences and redeem the emotions that were associated with those past events. This frees us emotionally by transforming how the ego closes us off to feeling some emotions while exaggerating others. When this occurs, the ego prevents us from accessing our intuition; and without that natural inner guidance, we are confused, depressed, and lost. Without our intuition intact, we experience inaccurate assessments of our emotions.

Dissolution "liquefies" our emotions so we can examine our relationship to them. When emotions begin to flow, the ego feels a threat to its existence and tries to pull us back under its control by making us ashamed or afraid of our emotions. We may feel anxious or fear our life is being threatened. But by observing courageously and without judgment, we can override the ego's influence. This is the meaning of the alchemical arcanum for Dissolution: "The way to truth is through Intelligence of the Heart." When the ego begins to come under our control, our hearts begin to feel safe enough to open to loving and being loved. You might envision the heart having an upper and a lower half. The lower represents the kind of love we equate with romance, and the upper represents spiritual love, unconditionality, and compassion. The work in Dissolution readies both halves for complete integration in the higher stages of alchemical transformation.

In laboratory alchemy, the alchemist dissolves the ash from Calcination in water. The dissolving of solids in water is like a return to the unborn state, in the transformational womb for eventual rebirth. The transformational water of Dissolution is not the physical water of our Earth or in our taps, but rather "a universal archetype, a nurturing, refreshing, flowing, feeling presence the ancient alchemists associated with the feminine, the waxing/waning, ever-changing, mystical powers of the moon that control the tides inside and outside our bodies."[1]

In Dissolution, the ego may make us feel like we're drowning in a large body of water—our emotions feel huge and overwhelm us. The ego fights to remove itself from this sea of emotions within which it believes it will lose control. It avoids association with anything it can't control. If we are brave enough to face the ego and its determination to keep us from our deeper emotions, we may gain support from our emotions themselves if we allow them to take us into greater depths of consciousness.

While you are deepening your process of Dissolution, you may feel fearful of the unknown. As the ego's rigid control is *temporarily* released (I emphasize *temporarily* because many such experiences are required before the creation of a new pattern of emotion becomes permanent), we may experience the underlying actions of the ego that were originally meant to protect our fragile aspects when we were young. We may come face to face with fear of feeling too much or too little, fear of revealing who we truly are, or fear of *being* who we truly are. The ego leads us to believe that if we reveal our authentic self, we will be somehow harmed, rejected, denied, criticized, or even annihilated.

Ego protections—such as an "I don't care" attitude, being cold and aloof, misusing our emotions to confuse and control others, putting on a "nice" girl (or boy) face, or rejecting the full range of our feelings just so we may remain "safe"—become obvious when Dissolution melts these defenses. We see that what we've rejected is an essential

---

1. Dennis William Hauck, *Alchemy Module One* (teaching materials), 40–41.

and important part of ourselves, and our feeling nature is what helps us redeem those denied aspects of being.

The stage of Dissolution requires the expression of emotion in order to redeem, or feel once again, our original emotional golden core. As a result, we can learn to discern the difference between our natural emotions and those we've used to protect, such as those believed by parents or society to be the only acceptable ones. This, of course, means different things to different people, so trying to be "acceptable" to others is a never-ending and self-defeating quest. The following meditation may assist you in accepting the value and beauty of your emotions.

The Magical Lake Meditation

Sit in a relaxed position, eyes closed, watching your breath, breathing lightly in and out. When you feel relaxed enough, imagine yourself in a beautiful place in nature—it could be somewhere you love to visit or someplace completely imaginary. Take time to look around you at everything there. Use your breathing to take you deeper into the meditation.

In the center of this scene, there is a lovely lake, surrounded by grasses and flowers. Your attention is drawn to the middle of the lake, where you see an elegant and ethereal water being emerging. She silently motions for you to enter the lake. You enter and she reaches for your hand.

Suddenly you are both deep underwater. You begin to panic but then realize you can breathe easily. You relax and she takes you to a small grotto filled with plants that wave in the current.

She tells you she is there to help you learn the value of your emotions. She asks you to begin telling her about the emotions that trouble you the most, one by one. After each, she tells you to be silent and think about how it would be if you didn't have that emotion. What would your life be like? What would your interactions or relationships with others be like? How would you express yourself if you didn't have this feeling?

Consider your answers to each of her questions, taking time to find the truest answer, and sharing it with her. If it is something positive, she will encourage it. If it is something negative, she gives you time to discover a better answer.

After you have shared all the emotions and discovered the wisdom within yourself about them, she tells you that from now on, you will have a different, more positive perception of your feelings.

Thank her and come back out of the lake to your starting point. Meditate on what you learned and then write in your journal.

⟫•◦•⟪

Have you ever wondered if you may have designed your life based upon what others think of your feelings and behaviors? Try to discover which ones are fear-based, which were learned, and which are healthy and natural. See if you can find feelings and behaviors that feel closely related to the Soul, such as love, determination, clarity of purpose, strength of character, serenity, compassion, and joy.

Authentic feeling is unconditional and without expectations. Ask yourself this: "If I were to love myself unconditionally, right here, right now, what would I have to give up in order to do this?" Be aware that this is a very difficult question! It holds no quick and easy answers. Before you nod and say that what you'd have to give up are your human emotions of rage, depression, or jealousy, the ones that you judge as "bad," look again. If unconditional love means accepting everything without judgment, then it must allow for our human experience of emotions in how they help us to evolve and awaken. The purpose of such emotions is to challenge and strengthen us in our resolve to grow and to seek the highest possible outcome of every experience. By bringing conscious awareness to all your emotions, you learn that it's okay to let go of those that no longer serve you or others in a positive way.

In research done by Michael Newton, Joel L. Whitton, Robert Schwartz, and others on the between-lifetimes states of consciousness, it has been found that a majority of hypnotherapy subjects report *feelings* as being a *necessary* part of the learning experiences between one lifetime and the next. When hypnosis subjects are taken to their lives between lives, their Soul state of beingness, many experience a "life review," as do many people who have had near-death experiences. In this review, the Soul looks at the life previously experienced. If it did anything to regret, it consequently must also feel the sorrow, remorse, or anger at having done so. Feelings help us make the changes required in order to evolve. The Soul may then choose to re-embody in the next lifetime in a way that corrects and rebalances the wrongs done in our previous lives. If the Soul chooses this, it further develops the gold within it.

When we run away from fearful feelings, and we are finally confronted by whatever it is that we've protected ourselves against, the thing itself is *never* as bad as fear had us believe. Many people feel amazed, and even a little foolish, at how much time, effort, and energy they put into hiding a feeling, only to discover that when reintegrated, they felt more whole. Many times, the fear of being annihilated by an emotion is the fear of feeling alive!

A film that explores this issue is *Everybody's Fine* (2009). The role played by Robert DeNiro exemplifies what can be done when we override our lifelong fear of emotion. In the film, DeNiro plays a mild-mannered and ineffective father in a family whose emotional range is vast, but also ineffective. The family members are either blaming one another for their problems, or hiding their "secrets" from their father in order to protect him and each other. When DeNiro decides to visit each of his four grown children, he begins to piece together what they are doing and sees himself reflected in their behavior. What he must overcome is his habit of closing himself off emotionally. The film ends after he becomes a model of loving and open communication who influences his family to do the same.

The film demonstrates clearly how much energy it takes to repress feelings and how ultimately destructive it is not to live with fully functioning emotions. Without them, we lose the riches that are within us because we've hidden from them for so long. The next exercise offers you a way to envision how this works.

REPRESSING EMOTIONS EXERCISE

Imagine that in front of you is a large container, such as a half wine barrel or large bucket, filled with water. Now imagine that for your *entire* life your task has been to submerge a large, fully inflated beach ball completely under the tub's water, not allowing any part of the ball to break the water's surface. How does your body feel as it exerts the effort necessary to hold that ball under water? How tired are you? How does it affect your mental outlook? How does it make you feel? Can you get on with your Soul's purpose and still keep that ball submerged? Do you even have the energy to consider why you've been doing this or any other important thing in your life?

—————

I'm sure you get the point. This analogy shows how much time, energy, effort, and false belief we put into hiding feelings that we've learned are unacceptable. The problem is that they're always there, just under the surface. We fear that in the millisecond it would take to succumb to the need for just a little break from the task of keeping the ball submerged, our emotions will come roaring up out of the tub, spilling over, obvious to anyone watching, and ruining our lives. Does this feel familiar?

Many times we suffer from painful emotions when they head in opposite directions—like an emotional tug of war. They represent the disconnected relationship between the conscious, or ego self, and the subconscious, or Soul self. This is a battle between our instinctual nature and our intellect, both of which have much to give, but not when they are in conflict. The resolution is to become conscious by eventually blending both instinct and intellect as if they're both floating peacefully on a sea of calm.

In the stage of Dissolution, we redeem and reintegrate our natural emotions, at the same time detaching from the associated historical events. The *emotion* connected to trauma or painful events often gets translated as just as bad as the event itself, so we repress those feelings in order to protect ourselves from re-experiencing the feelings in the original event. However, since our emotions are necessary and essential to our Soul's well-being, as well as being a way the Soul expresses itself, our feelings must be emancipated if we are to grow and mature spiritually. This is not a psychological process of digging up old traumas and reliving them, but rather redeeming the *feelings* that got stuck in the original event. In Dissolution we are reaching into a deep, dark well and discovering that there is clear, sparkling, and delicious water in its depths. The Dissolution arcanum at the beginning of this chapter tells us that the pathway to freedom and joy is through the heart. As you reach more deeply into your heart and discover its gifts, such as compassion, peace, and harmony, you discover new ways of experiencing emotion. The following meditation will help you to discover and embody your emotions more fully and authentically.

DISSOLUTION MEDITATION

Imagine yourself at the same cave as the one in the Calcination meditation. However, this time there is a deep, dark pool of water between you and the cave entrance. Your task is to find the courage to swim across the water, feeling your fears about the task, including anything your body bumps against as you swim! Allow your inner guidance to protect you.

As you reach the other side of the pool, climb out and enter the cave. Proceed to one of the alleyways that you see there, and read the signs on the doors. These signs identify a different emotion that you have always feared. Choose a door, knock on it, and if you are ready to pursue what lies within, the door will open. Explore the emotion in the room with an open mind and heart. If needed, ask your ego to suspend its protection for the moment so that you can experience the pure emotion and what it wants to teach you. You may discover here how your past beliefs and rigid ideas have held your natural emotions captive. (Just as in the Calcination meditation, be aware that your ego may resist letting go, so you may need to persist until it does.) When you are done, come back the same way you went in, open your eyes, and record your experiences in your alchemy journal.

—⇒◦⇐—

Feeling emotions is challenging to us all, no matter what context they may occupy. Certainly, strong emotion can be overwhelming. But the lack of emotion is "underwhelming," and we die to our true self, our potentials, and the gold within our Souls. This is why the stage of Dissolution can be so powerful and helpful—it demonstrates the value of emotion and how necessary it is to wholeness. Along with dreams being messages from our Souls, I believe emotion is one way our Souls guide us, helping us cleanse old ideas and beliefs, and build a stronger sense of self through unconditional love.

Summary Points

- Tears are important in the alchemical process since they contain salt, one of the three most important alchemical elements, and help us release issues from the past.
- Dissolution "liquefies" our emotions so we can feel their value and purpose.
- The ego tries to control our emotions, and this makes us ashamed or afraid of them, but by using the alchemical arcanum for Dissolution, "The way to truth is through the Intelligence of the Heart," we learn to listen to our emotions from the heart rather than the ego.
- While working with the water of Dissolution, it is not water as we know it—it is associated with deep feeling levels of being.
- By discovering lost emotions, we learn that these are the ones most closely related to our Soul—the ego protects us from these emotions because of their innate power.

- Running away from fear only worsens it until we are ready to confront whatever the fear is.

- When conflict between the intellect and our instinctual nature arises, we suffer difficult emotions. This is caused by a disconnect of the ego self and the Soul self. The resolution is to blend both instinct and intellect as partners.

- In Dissolution, we redeem and reintegrate our natural emotions while we detach from the emotions that were stuck in events of the past.

- Strong emotions are difficult, but the lack of emotion deadens our true potential. By working with Dissolution, we bring back the emotions that were held hostage in the past and can now use them fully and in the perfect way they were created to be.

CHAPTER 4

FROM FEAR TO FORTITUDE

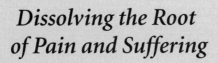

Dissolving the Root of Pain and Suffering

As you continue on your journey to transform beliefs that no longer serve and accept emotions you may have rejected in the past, it is important to keep in mind the underlying power of fear. The prevailing, underlying factor and cause of pain and suffering in *every* problem, challenge, or difficulty is *fear*, whether on a global or personal level. If you look closely at each, you will find an act of exclusion, an effort to reject, blame, or project onto others, and a battle *against* that which is feared, whether imagined or tangible, overt or disguised. This actually feeds fear and creates an ongoing cycle of belief in it. You can discover how fear permeates your life if you explore issues such as depression, overwork, criticism, anxiety, relationship problems, health challenges, etc. Look underneath the issue and you'll find fear. In the alchemical process of Dissolution, we come face to face with all of our emotions, and the most challenging is fear because it underlies all of our issues.

By merely having a strong desire to transform our lives, we have very little chance of creating permanent change if it is built upon rejection of uncomfortable material. This is like having a severe wound and pretending it doesn't exist just because it doesn't look nice—in the Arthurian legend, Sir Parsival ignores a king's wound because it makes the young knight feel uncomfortable. Certainly, it is difficult to face painful or frightening material. But when viewed from a Soul growth standpoint, we may choose to embrace the feelings involved in the challenge, as well as to recognize the wisdom and resolution available within the experience.

You can learn to recognize your own inner wisdom, the shining gold that is guided by your Soul. It requires facing your fears but with the intention of learning why they are present within you. Here is an exercise to help learn how fear affects your life, and what you can do about it by accessing the deepest parts of your fears, not with resistance, but with acceptance. Though the following exercise involves an elevator and not water, it is nevertheless a Dissolution experience because you are going deep down into your emotions, feeling them realistically, and coming back up knowing more about them than before.

RESOLVING FEAR EXERCISE

Try this: List all the challenges in your life that you feel hold you back, limit you, or prevent you from being who you'd like to be. From your list, take the most challenging one with you as you descend several floors in an elevator. As the elevator takes you down, stay aware of your intuitive-feeling sense since it is what will lead you to discover what's at the bottom of the elevator. As you step off on the lowest floor, still carrying that problem, look around you. What do you see? How do you feel?

Let's say you target your tendency to mistrust others' motivations and actions toward you. In looking for the underlying fear, you might find that your suspicions are a protection against intimacy with others, and under that is a fear that others might hurt you. Or you might discover that the deep feelings in relationship might cause you to lose control, leaving you vulnerable to what you fear about yourself and your ability to give and receive love.

If you don't feel at least a bit uncomfortable on this floor, get back on the elevator ... you got off too soon! There is yet a deeper level to reach. It is a dark floor that holds all of us prisoner, no matter what the problem is, be it personal or global, and its name is Fear.

Once you've reached the bottom level, and you know you are facing Fear itself, see if you can connect your challenge to its roots, such as fear of rejection; fear of not being good enough; fear of not knowing your purpose in life; fear of expressing your feelings; fear of having "bad luck" in relationships; fear of financial lack; fear of physical pain or attack; fear of your mortality, how your death will be, dying a painful death; fear based upon your belief that others are better than you; and the most potent of all—fear of the unknown. Allow yourself to feel each fear deeply—it will be a greater teacher for you than if you merely turn it into an intellectual exercise.

When you have an understanding of the greatest fear or fears within you, *without trying to get rid of it or making it "nice,"* take that understanding with you back up the elevator. Remember the old saying that knowledge is power. After you step off the elevator, be aware of how you feel and write it all down in your journal.

—————

The collective ego protects us from what we fear, and serves as a shield of strong belief against attempting to live a more authentic life. Some of us may dread that living a life of inner freedom means paying the price of releasing fears about what others think about us, and that would be too destabilizing. Some fear that by becoming authentic, behaving outside the "norm" or being wildly creative, will cause others to judge us as "crazy" or egotistical. It's painful to not fit in. As Kermit from *Sesame Street* sings, "It's not easy being green."

Think of this: Next time you find yourself being concerned about what another might think of you, good or bad, or when you long for someone's attention or recognition, stop, then pull your focus back to yourself. Find your center by first finding your feet and feeling your own energy; grounding is a quick and easy way to know where you are physically and emotionally. By projecting your own energy onto others through unfulfilled desires and expectations, you lose consciousness of yourself, as well as your connection to Earth, and you end up feeling lost, alone, and confused.

Not only do we project our energy onto others, but the reverse is true. This can affect us destructively if we are not conscious of it. Every time we allow verbal or physical abuse, the perpetrator's energies of rage enter into our own energy field. This energy, unless cleared, may stay with us for years—or an entire lifetime.

For anyone who has thought of themselves as a victim, there is no actual reality in being a victim. What looks like victimization is really our own fear-based and inaccurate perceptions of ourselves and the events in our lives. This weakens our beliefs about ourselves and leave us prey to those who spot the weaknesses and draw energy from us (sometimes called "energy vampires") through abuse and disrespect due to their own beliefs in victimization. When we allow outside influences and self-criticism to define our worth, it is hard to recognize the growthful opportunities that are presented to us, ones that offer freedom from those false perceptions. I've heard it said that "the strongest thoughtform wins," meaning that what we believe becomes our reality.

I love the scene in the 2008 film *The Secret Life of Bees* where Dakota Fanning's character as a young girl takes back her power from her abusive father as he is about to beat her, and yells at him that she's no longer afraid of him. As he stops and clearly considers what she's just done, he backs off. True power is identifiable and potent. In this scene, Fanning has combined Calcination, by burning out her ego-based fear, and Dissolution, where she blends it with the ashes from Calcination, and frees herself from further harm through expression of emotion.

You may be aware of studies done in large cities on how posture, carriage, and confidence powerfully affect whether the people in the study were mugged or not. Those who were not accosted carried a natural energy of, "I am not your victim so don't bother messing with me." This may sound too simple to be true, but just consider how the idea might reflect situations you've had in your life when, with a positive and confident perception of yourself, you came out stronger than before. This is the difference between believing yourself to be a victim or not. When we are immersed in victimization beliefs, we believe that our circumstances or other people prevent us from being, doing, saying, thinking, or feeling what we really want. We often use the word *can't*. The word actually means "I won't," which sounds like a petulant child. On the other hand, the words "I don't want to" can be self-supporting if not used as a defense but rather as a choice.

Just think of how free you'd feel if, instead of saying "I can't" to that annoying woman who keeps trying to recruit you for her latest fundraiser, you said truthfully, looking her straight in the eye, "No, thank you, I don't want to." (I hear you saying, "Whoa! I'm not sure I could do that!" And to that I say, "Yes, you can!")

Here's something you can do when your energy is drained by others or by your own limiting fears. This exercise will help you look at your fears and discover how to empower yourself by perceiving them differently than you usually do. We generally think the fear we're feeling has power over us and we can do nothing about it. But a powerful ritual like the one in this exercise will help you take your power back by expressing emotion so you are not controlled by fear. It is an exercise that helps you understand what Dissolution does in terms of freeing emotion.

DISEMPOWERING FEAR: EMPOWERING YOURSELF EXERCISE

(Best not to do this when others are around. You'll see why!) Clear everything out of your way, close the windows if need be, and stand up firmly in the center of the room. Ball up your fists, tighten all the muscles in your body, one at a time, hold the tension, then release. Do this a few times until you begin to feel something, even if what you feel is fear—*especially* if what you feel is fear!

Next, move your focus to your pelvic area. Feel it, sense it; imagine it as holding a large container of energy for you. Imagine bringing the energy up to your throat. Now growl (yes, I said growl!) loudly. Do this a few more times.

Then stand quietly and pay attention to how your body, emotions, and spirit feel. How is your energy level now? This technique helps you free up frozen energy, releases energy placed or even injected into your body by others, and puts you back into your natural energetic flow. Done regularly, this practice can transform and heal past traumas and abuse because it shifts the energy from one of victimization to natural empowerment.

———⪢◆⪡———

Each and every difficulty is meant for our evolvement and not proof of our unworthiness. Somewhere we may have gotten the idea that life was supposed to be easy, and when we find that is not always true, we collapse inward and believe we've done it wrong. This perception creates an attitude of defeat, which adds to the construction of a strong belief in failure as a person.

A negative phrase used by so many is "I'll believe it when I see it." What if we turned it around and said instead, "I'll see it when I believe it." When we are willing to accept our challenges for the potentials they hold for us, we can transform destructive behaviors and experience.

The story of Vincent Astor is a good example of how someone overcame strong opposition and disempowering rejection by family, and became a servant of humanity. The wealthy and privileged Astor family had held great power in the United States and Europe for over two hundred years. Vincent, as a member of this famous family, was called "the ugly one" by his mother, who rejected him completely from the day of his birth. His father, the John Jacob Astor who died on the *Titanic*, disciplined him harshly, further dismissing Vincent by making it clear that he was the family outcast.

Until Vincent grew up and began his career as a humanitarian, none of the Astors had ever given of themselves or their fortune in service to others. Vincent was the first Astor to donate to charity and give back in many other ways to his beloved city of New York. Because of his hellish upbringing and relentless rejection, when most people would have given up and turned to various vices and self-abuse, Vincent believed he was more than his family believed him to be. He never accepted his family's attitudes about himself, and as a result, he was able to develop compassion for the human collective.

Here is an example of how I discovered one way in which fear played a role in my life. When I began my moon cycles (menses) at twelve years old, I began to be plagued by periodic migraine head-aches. They were devastating and continued well into adulthood. Pain relievers didn't touch the throbbing ache and nausea; doctors just told me I'd "grow out of it." Whenever I'd get the foreshadowing indicator of flashing geometric shapes in my vision, my heart would sink since I knew what was to follow.

One day, in my thirties, I was visiting a good friend when the frightening light show and graphic shapes began to appear in my line of vision. I immediately took two ibuprofen tablets and asked if I could lie down. My friend showed me his guest room and I lay on the waterbed, praying for the migraine not to materialize. I realized how frightened I was, so I calmed myself down by breathing rhythmically and feeling the subtle motion of the water (relating to how Dissolu-tion can change our perceptions) in the bed. I looked up at the ceiling, and in my altered vision, I was able to watch the psychedelic lights that flashed in geometric patterns. I became quite fascinated with this light show, and realized that I'd always been so afraid of what was to follow that I'd never paid attention to this amazing experience.

Intuitively, I was guided to ask my body to release its need to create a migraine, and instead to reveal to me what was causing the headaches. I told my body that if it could do that for me, I would promise to deal as consciously as possible with whatever problem I had been ignoring, and was causing the migraines. My promise felt deep and authentic, and as I settled into it, drawing upon my courage to allow change to happen, the light show began to diminish and the headache never occurred. Within about fifteen minutes, I was able to get up from the bed and go out to enjoy the day with my friend. From that moment on, whenever I suspected the onset of a migraine, I'd lie down, relax into a consciousness of no fear, reaffirm my prom-ise, and listen carefully to what my body, emotions, and spirit wanted me to pay attention to. Within a year or so, I was never bothered by migraines again.

Let's look at a hypothetical event that could happen to anyone. You've just heard that your company is being downsized. You can choose to perceive this as a threat to your very existence and fall into a mire of paralyzing fear, or you can choose to see this as an opportunity. (The Chinese glyph for *crisis* means "opportunity.") To do this, however, you have to access two things within yourself: honesty and courage (from the French *coeur*, meaning "heart"). This is difficult because so many of us don't always tell ourselves the truth for fear we don't know the truth. Inner courage may be difficult to access and apply when we are challenged, but it is nevertheless inherent within us all.

So in this scenario, you can choose, instead of freezing with fear, to inquire within how you really feel about your job. This might be the perfect time to use a Dissolution meditation, where you communicate with your feelings and attain truth. Perhaps you never really liked the job. If so, the elimination of your job is a gift that frees you to move on to what you truly want to do. But maybe you genuinely love your job, and what you discover when you courageously retrieve your true feelings is that very love. Perhaps by bringing that feeling more actively to the surface, it may begin to radiate from you. Perhaps it gets noticed by administrators who may decide you won't be an employee they lay off. Even if you were to lose that job, trusting the love within you could bring you to a new, even more satisfying way to work in the world. This is very different than what happens when you succumb to your fears. It's hard work to maintain faith in a positive outcome and not be fearful, but with honesty and courage on your side, amazing things will happen because you created them with your change of perception.

Say these words aloud, all of which are synonyms for courage, and *feel* how they affect you: dauntlessness, heart, mettle, guts, pluck, resolution, spirit, spunk, audacity, boldness, bravery, fearlessness, valor, nerve, backbone, self-assurance, daring. John Wayne once defined courage as "being scared to death and saddling up anyway."

Between the ages of thirty and fifty, I engaged in various tests of my courage by doing class four and five whitewater river-rafting expeditions, camping alone, and going on solo vision quests. In one of these quests, I planned to spend the night in what felt to be an ancient shaman's cave at a location in New Mexico. I packed in a few essentials, all the while avoiding questioning looks from tourists who were leaving before it got dark.

Once at the cave, I settled myself in the entrance and sat watching the sunset and distant thunderstorm, which was approaching fast. I could feel the moisture in the air and it felt supercharged. My attention was on the drawings on the walls of the cave, and I asked permission to be there of the ancient spirit people who had been there long before me. I closed my eyes and began to meditate. I felt secure, and deeply moved by the privilege of being in this place. I began to hear drops of rain closing in. Suddenly I heard a whooshing sound and felt something swiftly skate through my hair. It happened again. Trying to understand what had just happened, I was afraid I had disturbed the ancient spirits, and they didn't want me there. So I grabbed my daypack and flashlight and began to exit the cave. As I stood up, I saw the creatures who had flown through my hair on their way into the cave: bats! As I breathed a sigh of relief that it wasn't angry spirits after all, I became aware of the storm, which by then was much closer and stronger. I walked hurriedly to my car about a half mile away, only later to realize that I had been walking not on the marked trail, but along the very edge of a high cliff!

After I returned to my lodgings, I reviewed what had happened and I realized I had gone on this quest with my ego telling me that because I was somehow special, I would be recognized by the spirits of the cave and a profound and enlightening experience would be offered to me. This image hovered in the back of my mind and contributed to my other belief that, because I *was* special, I wouldn't be afraid. I thought of myself as particularly courageous because I was a young woman and most women wouldn't think of doing what I was embarking upon.

As I pondered the experience, I looked up at the bookshelf. I was drawn to a book about New Mexico and pulled it off the shelf. While leafing through it, I was stunned by a photograph of a thunderstorm with this caption: "Every year many people are killed in New Mexico by lightning strikes while sitting in the mouth of caves." I burst out laughing and knew what would have happened if not for those little bats! I laughed even harder when I realized that I'd been pretending to be courageous, when in fact I was terrified. But even though I could see myself as a very vulnerable human being, that golden, intuitive part within me had guided me safely back. I realized later that what I'd been believing was courage was merely hope—and what I could then recognize as authentic courage was within my inner guidance system, my intuition. This had been a Dissolution experience by combining the ashes from my calcified ego with the water and fire essences of the approaching storm. My ego had tried to keep me under its control with fear, but my deep intuitive self knew what to do and called forth my inner courage. This could only happen because I'd deflated my ego by acknowledging I wasn't ready for this adventure.

On another of my solo vision quests, this time at 11,000 feet in the mountains of Colorado, I learned a new way of perceiving. My experiences on this quest clearly demonstrated how it was my *perceived* experience, not the actual one, that created my fear.

Just as darkness began to fall, I finished my prayers for protection and guidance in the inner journey I was about to take. Looking up, I spied an eagle soaring high above, stunningly backlit by the sunset. It circled round and round, and I took this to be a good omen.

I settled down, leaned my back against a pine tree, drank some water, and continued to meditate. Several minutes passed, and because I had fasted for twenty-four hours in preparation for what I hoped would be a guiding vision, I began to see, hear, and feel things that indicated that I was no longer in my ordinary awareness. This was better than I had hoped!

After what seemed like hours, I was suddenly jolted back to an awareness of something on my left shoulder making an ominous scratching noise. I just knew it had to be a claw of something huge and deadly! I leapt up, bumping my head on a tree branch and frantically rocketing around the circle of protection I had drawn in the dirt when I arrived. I began making karate-like moves (though I had no experience in the practice) and yelling at whatever had attacked me to leave me alone.

When I calmed down, I felt I had failed myself as a woman of courage. I sat down against the tree, took some deep breaths, and reaffirmed my intention to stick it out no matter what. I drank more water and resumed my meditation.

I went quickly back into a deep state of consciousness and began having visions of animals, people, events, known and unknown, in psychedelic colors and accompanying unearthly sounds. As my absorption with these visions intensified, awareness of my body ceased, and I began to expand outward into the fields of energy surrounding my physical body. I was just barely aware that I was sitting on an 11,000-foot mountaintop with no human around for miles. I felt a shift in awareness from fear to assurance, even after having been told by the locals that bears, mountain lions, and bobcats had been spotted recently in the exact area in which I was questing. It had seemed to me that there was far less to fear from the extant animal life than if humans had been around.

As I sunk deeper and deeper into expanded consciousness, I wasn't prepared to hear and feel once again the scratching on my left shoulder, this time more loudly than before. Yet because I was in such a deep state, I was able to access a higher part of my consciousness that would offer a different perception. I slowly turned my face toward my left shoulder, feeling a combination of fear and deep peace. As I focused on my shoulder, I saw, in the moonlight, nothing more than a little mouse. It was sitting there, most likely wanting to cozy up for the night.

I burst out laughing, which was an extraordinary sound due to my expanded condition. It was like someone else was doing the laughing, which made me laugh even harder.

I thanked the little mouse for showing me how my internal programming had led me to believe it was a saber-toothed tiger tapping me for its dinner when, in fact, it had been a charming little teacher who taught me the importance of gaining courage through inner peace.

In his book *Your Soul's Plan*, author Robert Schwartz writes: "To heal fear we need to experience it—resistance to any energy only makes it stronger—and then choose to move beyond it."[2]

As we decide to grow past our old fears, the ego-protector may reemerge, seeming to threaten our very existence if we dare attempt to break free of its protection. As it thrashes around, stirring up fear and mayhem, our inner work begins to look impossible. It is so daunting that some of us may regress to relying once again on the ego-protector, and we go back to living our lives, fearing much and never feeling the fresh winds of freedom.

In Dissolution, you may engage in a war of emotions, either within yourself or with someone in your life. This may play out when you finally speak up after a long pattern of biting your tongue. Aha! Here's where some really potent fear resides! It's an opportunity to see how we convince ourselves *not* to speak our minds, *not* to express our artistic talents, *not* to go for that dream job. And why *not*? Because others might not like it. They might reject us. They might gossip about us behind our backs. My definition of a gossip is someone who lives vicariously and gutlessly through others.

Until I learned to accept my emotions so I could speak up for myself and others, my life was filled with confusion. I spent hundreds of hours and dollars in therapy delving into why I wasn't fulfilling my potential. I believed adversity was an unnecessary detour and not part of what I thought should be my plan. It felt like my party was continually being spoiled. I knew I held negative beliefs about myself, but they all seemed unrelated except for their persistent effects on my life. I assumed the reasons for all my problems were as varied as the problems themselves. I had no idea there was a key linking them all together, and that key lay in the strength of my ego-based fears.

I've been offering transformational work since the 1970s, and what I came to discover about fear emerged through many years of observing and sensing deeply into the difficulties confronting my students. As with my own process, I originally began working with

---

2. Robert Schwartz, *Your Soul's Plan* (Berkeley, CA: Frog Books, 2009), 123.

their issues as having multiple causes. Obviously, this was hard for them and hard for me as well. It was like fishing for a whole variety of underwater creatures with several poles at one time. What I didn't see then was that there was only one rather large fish at the bottom of the pond hiding under a lot of muck and mire; and, of course, it was a very clever fish. First, its weight snapped the lines and then the poles, too. The result: frustration, a feeling of defeat, and an assumption that I'd need to find another pond and much more expensive tackle.

But often, the fish would barely raise his head to the surface, just enough to seduce me into staying with that pond, at the same time trying to scare me away by its size and appearance. Then it would snuggle its way deep down into the slime at the bottom of the pond so that my sonar couldn't detect the presence of anything viable in my search. Once I finally stopped whipping my line around in the water in my attempt to discover what was making all that fuss in the pond, the water began to clear. When it did, I came face to face with the origin of all species of suffering: fear. By then I had collected enough experience to know the habits of that big ol' fish. I also began suspecting that it wouldn't be so big and fat if it weren't getting fed by my belief in it.

The truth behind that suspicion began emerging as I tested one of my theories, which was based upon the simple alchemical-metaphysical principle: like attracts like. Again, the apt example is, when we listen to and believe what the news media has to say, we create our realities. When NBC announces we are in a recession, guess what happens pretty quickly? Bingo! Money seems to get tight. Costs rise. Homes go into foreclosure. The homeless population increases.

How does this happen? By *believing* that we have no power over, and refusing to take any responsibility for, what we think about the big fish. Our fear-based belief is like a negative magic that hypnotizes us into unconsciousness, and voilà! We've created the very thing we've learned to be afraid of. The key here is seeing that our beliefs are merely stimulated or triggered, not *caused*, by an outer authority, be it the president, a newscaster, a preacher, or our parents.

Just as we can create reality in negative ways, we can also create positive, life-enhancing experiences—not by rejecting parts of ourselves or our lives, but by *including* them as rich fodder for growth. With unconditional acceptance of all aspects of ourselves, and with an intention to understand what they are teaching us, we create healthy, life-affirming realities.

This passage from Dan Brown's *The Lost Symbol* illustrates my point:

> What if I told you that a *thought*... any tiny idea that forms in your mind ... actually has *mass*? What if I told you that a thought is an actual *thing*, a measurable entity, with a measurable mass? ... What are the implications?
>
> Well, the obvious implications are ... if a thought has mass, then a thought exerts gravity and can pull things toward it.[3]

When it comes to our thoughts about ourselves, a belief in worthlessness and self-loathing only creates more of the same, inwardly and outwardly. Friends drop away and jobs are lost as confirmation of these powerful attitudes toward self. Our perception of ourselves as valueless becomes a powerful and self-perpetuating icon of our belief and behavior.

Exhibiting confidence and success can be just the other side of the same coin unless held within a balanced understanding of the relationship between the light and dark aspects of ourselves. From this balance springs true strength, power, creativity, and connectivity to our golden spiritual core.

The more we believe in our limitations and unworthiness, the more they expose what we fear. The woman who meekly accepts a secondary position at work when she is the most qualified person for the job announces that she disavows her skills. Why should she be considered for a better position when she energetically broadcasts, "I'm not good enough!" The more we strongly confirm our negative beliefs about ourselves and our conditions, the more firmly entrenched they

---

3. Dan Brown, *The Lost Symbol* (New York: Doubleday, 2009), 78.

become, and the more they become our reality. Conversely, as we dissolve the ego's influence and limitations, we can choose to see clearly how our attitudes and beliefs about ourselves create our reality. This is where *Separation,* the third stage of transformational alchemy, comes in. It is the level of inner work that assists us in discovering how powerful our thoughts are, and which ones have either pulled us away from our purpose and indwelling confidence or supported us in fulfilling our lives. Separation teaches us how to use our mental capacity to discern what these negative and positive influences have been and how we can change them. It's an opportunity to move closer to the precious gold that lies within us.

Summary Points

- Fear is the root of all problems and challenges, personally and globally.

- Many people choose not to work with fear because of what others may think.

- Being a victim is based upon our fear-based and inaccurate perceptions of ourselves. And this leaves us vulnerable to others' criticisms, which contributes to our belief in victimization.

- Using strong emotions wisely to protect ourselves frees us from harm. Positive perceptions of ourselves, combined with grounded emotions, can protect us.

- Using a true expression of your feelings empowers you, such as when you say, "No, thank you, I don't want to," rather than doing something you really don't want to do.

- Adversity leads us to authenticity and freedom by showing us our strengths when we overcome fear.

- We can choose to perceive a challenge as an opportunity rather than a crisis that we can't do anything about.

- Finding courage involves *integrating* the power of the ego, not killing it off or trying to get rid of it. Integration of the ego brings it under our control and we can use its power and energy to assist us.

- Dissolution helps us transform our reaction to our life situations—it teaches us that our emotions are not bad, and that we can learn to speak up for ourselves and accomplish whatever we've dreamed of.

- We fool ourselves when we think each of our issues has multiple causes. The truth is that there is only one cause of difficulty: fear. And the resolution to transforming fear into fortitude is to not "feed" it by believing it's the truth when, in fact, it's an illusion.

- Just as we can create negative experiences with our thinking, we can also create positive ones.

- What we believe about ourselves manifests outwardly in our lives.

CHAPTER 5

SEPARATION

How Our Perceptions Create Our Reality

*"Every created thing carries
the signature of its creator."*
~ALCHEMICAL ARCANUM THREE

The arcanum for *Separation* is an alchemical principle that teaches us that thoughts—and perceptions of those thoughts—create what we experience as our reality. In alchemy, the stage of Separation sorts out and detaches us, through discernment and a blossoming wisdom, from old habits, beliefs, and behaviors that have been brought to consciousness in the first and second stages of Calcination and Dissolution. Separation is the important interim stage between the burning out and dissolving of old material and the next stage of Conjunction, where what has been discovered and separated comes together again in a new configuration of consciousness. Whenever we pull anything apart to discover what it is and how it works, we are doing the work of Separation. Doing this on inner levels is analogous to the work of writing a new job description for your ego-protector, which engages the intellect in defining and organizing what we most need to change in order to grow. (See "Writing a New Job Description for Your Ego-Protector" in appendix B.) Alchemist Dennis William Hauck tells us, "The purpose of Separation is the classification and analysis of previously hidden material by the rational mind to extract a person's essence ... dissecting and discarding what is no longer relevant or useful is the important goal of the Separation process."[4]

Ask yourself what beliefs, attitudes, and behaviors need to be sacrificed, separated from, and released from your life on physical, mental, emotional, and spiritual levels? The work of *Separation* helps you answer this question by revealing what serves you and what doesn't. This is a level of mental exploration, but is not an intellectual hiding when upsetting emotions arise. Rather, it is a place where we deepen understanding of our emotions, defenses, and behaviors in order to change our responses when challenges arise, and align ourselves more closely with our Soul's purpose.

---

4. Dennis William Hauck, *The Emerald Tablet* (New York: Penguin Books, 1999), 202.

In alchemy, as in shamanism and depth psychology, we go through processes that make us feel as though we're being dismembered, piece by piece. The process of Separation assists in freeing ourselves from old concretized beliefs that no longer portray our reality. We do this by calling forth our higher self, which separates the less conscious self in preparation for whatever wants to emerge from a deeper realization of consciousness. It may feel like a death, but it's the old ways dying, while we are being prepared to be reborn as our authentic, golden self.

Separation teaches us how to discern, a more advanced use of the intellect that, untended, rejects emotion and disconnects us from Soul in favor of logic. Our Souls express through our emotions, so when we intellectually dismiss our feeling nature, we sever access to our Soul. Great artists, writers, musicians, and other highly expressive, sensitive people could not create if their feeling natures were not accessible.

By being aware of our feelings and learning to make decisions that support their healthy expression, we no longer block them, and in so doing, open access to our Soul. Repressed creativity, like denied feelings, can lead to a variety of problems, physically, emotionally, and spiritually. It takes a lot of courage to face taboo areas. It is far easier to stay in a bad relationship or to continue working for the same abusive boss than it is to leave. Leaving, quitting, and making important changes can be terrifying. We fear that we won't be able to support ourselves financially and emotionally. We hang on by our wobbly hopes that somehow things will get better. But most of us have tried that enough times to know it never works.

Beliefs that are built upon inaccurate perceptions of ourselves, such as the idea that we have a helpless little child within us, keep us from the truth of spiritual maturation. By separating, sorting out, and pulling apart our old beliefs, we are more likely to disengage from old ideas and take the new pathway that frees us. Here is a ritual you can use to support your intention to let go of the old and open to the new.

Releasing Ritual

There is a definite power in ritual. You can perform a simple but effective Separation ritual that involves a symbolic sacrifice of what has supported a dependency on something or someone you need to release. This ritual may be as simple as lighting two candles that represent you and the person or situation you wish to liberate. Tie a silver or gold cord to both candles and place them in a safe place, such as a bathtub. Then begin speaking from the heart as if you were facing that person or situation about your reasons for ending your relationship—at least how it's been in the past. When you have said everything you need to say, cut the cord between the candles to symbolize release. Let the candles burn down completely overnight. When determination of mind and strong emotion combine with a willingness to allow higher forces to be in control, the energy of what was no longer serving you is transformed.

━━◆◆━━

During the second alchemical stage of Dissolution, we utilize strong emotion to make contact with deeper parts of ourselves that the ego has prevented us from exploring. In the stage of Separation, the ego has been temporarily brought under control and allows us entry into a deeper perception of our feeling nature as related to Soul. We have all had experiences in which we were frightened by the intensity of our feelings, and may have escaped to the intellect, thinking that it would protect us and even "get rid of" those pesky emotions. Has that ever really worked? Using the intellect in this way is actually a *misuse*. The higher purpose of the intellect is to complement emotional states. It is the marriage of the left-brain forces of the intellect with the right-brain forces of feeling and intuition. The task is not to outdo or overshadow the other, but rather to perform the sublime dance of surrender to the other. It is the entry into the *hieros gamos*, or "sacred marriage," which takes place at the fourth stage of alchemical transformation, Conjunction. Our experiences in the process of Separation increase our capacity for whole perceptions, including rather than excluding. This frees us to make decisions based upon new perceptions, without judgment or fear, because we are no longer limited.

Here is a meditation that illustrates how what you think becomes your reality and how, by consciously exploring and observing your thoughts, you can change that reality. By using the intellect to separate out thoughts, habits, or patterns, you can more clearly define the reality you are creating.

SEPARATION MEDITATION

Imagine yourself sitting quietly in a deep cave, eyes closed. Ask your inner guidance to show what you need to know to find a resolution to a current problem.

Now, imagine two closets just inside the cave entrance. Inside the closet doors are shelves filled with various objects. There is a difference between the contents of the two closets: one houses things that represent the old ways that you have always used to solve problems, some effective, some not; the other closet contains new ideas, new concepts, new possibilities. The objects in the closets are symbolic representations of these ways. An example might be a small statue of a bull if you've usually handled difficult people by bullying. In the other closet, you might find a crystal heart to represent your intention to attend to challenges in a more open-hearted way.

Intuitively choose a few items from each closet. Sit on the ground and spread the items out in front of you, keeping the items that symbolize the old ways separate from the ones that offer new ways.

Set a strong, clear intention to learn what these items can teach you. Ask your question again, clearly and with strong intent. Let your hands move toward whichever item or items provide the answer you need. You may be surprised about what the items tell you. A key is not to avoid or reject the ones you don't like—those will usually be the most revealing ones.

When you feel complete, come back out of the cave in the same way you went in, open your eyes, and write the insights in your journal.

———◆———

The alchemical arcanum for Separation, "Every created thing carries the signature of its creator," tells us that it is up to us whether we create our lives based upon our fears or what we sense as our higher potential. Either way, our life experiences correspond to whatever we think, whatever we believe.

Picture this: A child psychologist looks through a large observation window into a room where there is a huge pile of manure. Children enter the room, one at a time, and the therapist observes their behavior.

The first child goes in, looks around, and starts crying and calling for its mother.

The second child enters and begins angrily throwing handfuls of manure at the walls.

When it is the third child's turn, she digs in enthusiastically, getting much obvious joy from the task. Curious, the psychologist goes in and asks the child what she's doing. The little girl replies, "With so much of this in here, I know there must be a pony in it somewhere!"

Modern quantum physicists have taught us that human observation of the actions of certain objects, such as atoms, causes those actions to change. But in the process of observation, the scientists *also* experience changes within themselves. Some quantum physicists, like their alchemist predecessors, have courageously postulated that there appears to be a component of spiritual consciousness within physical life. They, too, are working with the concept that our perceptions create our reality and our reality confirms our perceptions.

As we proceed on the razor's edge of transformational work, our friends may grumble that we just aren't the same as we used to be.

They, like our ego-protectors, try to lure us back to the old ways in order that *they* may be comfortable again, or if this doesn't work, they may even disappear from our lives. As previously unchallenged beliefs begin to dissolve, we feel lost and afraid because justification for remaining the same is being extinguished. This can be a frightening time.

Painful experiences are common and necessary if our resistance to change is deeply entrenched. It hurts to pull out a deeply implanted thorn, but allowing it to remain is to create a festering wound. Some of us conclude that it's best never to become conscious, for it's too dangerous, too threatening, too risky. We fear the changes it would bring about in our lifestyles. This fear of change often prevents us from knowing that our outer life may not necessarily change but our *perception* of it does. If we feel negatively about our job, for instance, we create an atmosphere around us at work that demonstrates our misery. In the same way, an attitude that radiates confidence and self-acceptance creates a positive response.

Let's take a look at a good example of how this balance of forces within us can work to advantage. In psychology, there is a condition called a "complex." If you have ever been told you have one of these, you probably felt pretty nervous. But if we refer to *Webster's Dictionary*, we can begin to repurpose the concept from its psychiatric definition. The dictionary says this about *complex*: "a weaving or twining together, to encircle or embrace, consisting of two or more related parts, involved, complicated, intricate, not simple; made up of many elaborately interrelated or interconnected parts, so that much study or knowledge is needed to understand or operate it."

We are *complex* beings, intricately involved systems of consciousness, and an important part of the Divine Mystery. Expanding our perceptions and accepting ourselves warts and all is a most dynamic way to begin to remember our true purpose. Our "complexity" may be one of the gifts that lead us to consciousness.

I once presented a dream to two friends, one a metaphysical minister and the other a conservative and traditional psychotherapist, both of whom work with dreams. In the dream, I am living and working in a huge, multistoried building—a *complex*. There are many significant people there from my past. The building-complex is being demolished in order to be rebuilt in another location to which I seem to be going. I am on ground level watching the process. There is a huge snakelike sculpture made of paper and wood that contains symbolic objects from my past. It is old and crumbling and hanging from the building. A woman is pulling it down. I start to walk away, saying goodbye to all my friends. As I leave, I observe all the pain and suffering of my life displayed before me. I enter an asylum (dictionary definition: "a sanctuary, a place of retreat and safety"), where an orderly, a gentle young man, encourages me to explore my feelings and he keeps me safe while I do so.

My therapist friend was concerned and felt the dream heralded an approaching emotional breakdown. My minister friend laughed and congratulated me on dreaming about freedom. I believe both friends were right. The dream announced a period of redesigning my life, which required the dismantling, or *breaking down*, of old beliefs that no longer served me, so I could *break through* to where I needed to be. As the dream foretold, some friends drifted away and new ones, more in alignment with who I had become, came into my life. The most important part of the dream, however, helped me become appreciative of how *complex* I was.

By not valuing our multiple inner resources and uniqueness, and by becoming immersed in the belief that a problem has only one solution, we limit possibilities. When we rise above the problem and expand into multiple possibilities, we can see the whole picture and make wiser decisions based upon discernment rather than judgment.

Many of us have difficulty in trusting others. When we have expectations that others will be the ways we want them to be, we put conditions on their behaviors and responses to us. This colors how we respond to them and affects how we feel about ourselves as well. Yet it's not up to others to fulfill our expectations. It's up to us to refrain from putting conditions on them. We place similar conditions on ourselves: "I can't accept that job offer because I'm not educated enough," "I can't date anyone until I lose this weight," "I can't draw because I can't do it perfectly," "I can't do all this transformational stuff because it's too scary!"

Did you notice all the "can't's"? "Can't" is just a false front for "I don't want to," "I won't," or, more accurately, "I'm afraid." Look at the "I can'ts" in the preceding paragraph and substitute the words "I'm afraid." Feel the difference? Try applying this exercise in all the times you say "I can't" during a week's time—you'll be surprised. You'll learn a great deal if you take note of the fear that may be underneath the words.

How we perceive others affects how we create our own suffering or freedom. If we have someone (or a situation) in our lives that always irritates us, and we're always upset when they come to mind, it probably indicates that we have a perception of them that doesn't fit our expectations.

For example, how do you feel about the following statement? *I can trust everyone to be exactly who they are in every moment.* What are your resistances to this statement? Are you thinking of exceptions that make you feel you wouldn't be able to apply this? Like your abusive uncle? Or obnoxious neighbor? Yet these people in particular prove the value of the statement. You *can* trust your uncle to be exactly who he is in every given moment, whether he's a drunk or merely flakey and unreliable. You can trust him to be that or anything else within the context of who he is. You set yourself up for disappointment when you choose to think of him *not* being who he is, but rather who you wish him to be. This is not his reality. Yours is healthier when you don't cloud your perceptions of your uncle with judgments and expectations outside his reality.

Our task isn't that we should naively trust everyone to be *good* to us, or to act in the ways we want them to. Instead, before we pre-judge anyone—or ourselves—we use the idea that *everyone is whoever they are at whatever times, no matter what we think or do about it.* In so doing, we are freed to make decisions based upon what *is* rather than what we *expect.* If we have unrealistic expectations, our reality reflects that back to us in some way. If we let go of conditions, we create a reality that supports how we want to live our lives.

Changing our minds about ourselves and living on the vanguard of this new thinking takes courage, because it challenges centuries of fear and negative belief. For an individual to disengage from society's limitations and rules of conduct takes clarity of purpose and a willingness to risk it all by discovering and *being* a unique individual, authentically oneself.

Expanding your perceptions of reality by changing your beliefs from negative to positive and detaching from limited ways of thinking can be challenging. Here are some simple ideas to try in your practice of freeing yourself into a more positive way of being. They set up a positive habit pattern that can help you to "stop, look, and listen" when you hear yourself thinking in a negative fashion.

FIVE EXERCISES TO FREE OLD HABITS

1. Be selective in the music you listen to. Don't just mindlessly listen to a radio station. Try listening to different stations, ones that challenge you. For example, if you've always hated classical music, try it! Choose music that matches your taste but frees your beliefs by stretching your boundaries.

2. If you choose to watch TV, get a DVR (digital video recorder) so that you can record the programs you like, then fast-forward through the commercials instead of letting them hypnotize you into conforming to what others want you to believe and buy.

3. Question your shopping habits. Do you *have* to have that dress? Or could you remodel an older one in your closet in a way that makes it unique to *you* and offers you the opportunity to be creative? Is it really necessary to buy holiday gifts for every person you know? Could you hand-make gifts so that they come from your heart instead of your wallet? Could you give a card rather than a gift, with a note promising to spend quality time with your friend?

4. Try this: Instead of engaging in mindless chatter with friends, ask them if they'd be willing to go on a silent walk with you in

nature. If they are willing, great! What friends! But if not, go by yourself and enjoy the gift of solitude.

5. Do the unexpected. You can get really creative with this one! If your family usually argues and grumbles about after-dinner chores, such as washing the dishes, try making a chart with everyone's name on it as well as numbered chores. Then, before anyone begins to eat, they each have to roll a die and whatever number they get is their chore. Depending on the size of your family, you can leave one or two numbers blank, which will give some members a night off. A special rule on the chart can be something like, whoever doesn't do their chore gets a surprise. And the surprise can be something like putting the unwashed pots and pans on the culprit's bed the next day after they've left for school or work!

———⟹◆⟸———

As we change perceptions of ourselves, we reconsider experience from a wider spectrum of consciousness. We discover strengths and talents we never thought we had, and can also identify how we abdicated authenticity for acceptability. The choices we make from new perceptions ground us in who we truly are. Through the process of Separation, we've learned that what we've always believed may not be true—or at least not fit who we are now.

In the next chapter, you'll learn more about how we are always making choices so our Souls can evolve and we can move closer to our own Philosopher's Stone.

Summary Points

- Alchemical principles teach that thoughts and perceptions create what we experience.
- The alchemical mental stage of Separation helps us find and understand which thoughts, habits, beliefs, and behaviors need to be further processed after the first two stages.

- By asking how a situation, challenge, or experience serves us and our process, we gain knowledge from a positive, life-affirming standpoint, rather than being held hostage by a negative belief.

- Some of the work we do in Separation is a dismemberment of all that we previously held to be true. This separates us from our past and how we habitually reacted to it.

- Separation teaches us to *discern*, rather than judge, situations and ourselves.

- How we perceive a situation defines whether we suffer from it or use it to help us grow.

- As we separate ourselves from the ego's negative influence, we may suffer the pain of friends moving away from us when they see us changing—this is due to their fear of having to make changes themselves.

- When we fear the changes we're going through, it's a dis-illu-sion-ment—our old beliefs are being pulled apart and burned or dissolved. And that can be frightening because we don't know yet where we'll end up.

- Trying to find out what's *wrong* with you will never work—but you will succeed if your intention is to find out what's *right* with you.

- Learning to accept your complexities is one of the ways to loving yourself unconditionally.

- By changing your perceptions of yourself and the world, you contribute to changing others in positive ways.

- Separation teaches us that what we've always believed to be true may not be, at least not anymore. It gives us the opportunity to create new beliefs that "fit" us better.

CHAPTER 6

CHOOSING OUR REALITIES

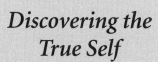

Discovering the True Self

W e learn in Separation how our thoughts and beliefs have great
power to create our lives, either negatively or positively. We
gain aspects of self that we were unaware of before, and can begin
sorting out how we wish to live our lives from this point. Through
dissecting our thoughts, beliefs, and attitudes we found in Separation,
we learn how to bring the higher consciousness together with the
lower. An alchemical maxim that runs through the entire work is "As
above, so below," which means whatever we experience in the earthly
realm is found in the heavenly realm—and vice versa. When our personal alchemical transformation reaches a degree where we can apply
what we learn about ourselves to the universe, we move closer to unification with the Divine. This means there is no separation, no difference, no disconnection between the upper and lower realms. There
are not two realities, earthly and spiritual—they are both part of the
same consciousness and essence.

In our exploration of the unity of all life is the concept of the eter-
nality of everything created by a higher power. If we, as creations of
that power, are part of the everything else in life, then we must be
eternal ourselves. This gives us the chance to experience successive
lifetimes, and this gives us the opportunity to seek out experiences
that assist our Souls in evolving. And between lifetimes, before we are
born into yet another life, our Souls make choices for the upcoming
life that will help them to grow. This is how we can experience the
alchemical statement of "As above, so below." What we learn while in
an earthly life we bring to our between-lifetime experience. And what
we learn between lifetimes we bring to our earthly life. The following
story, though fictional, illustrates how challenging this concept of pre-
birth choices and agreements between Souls can be for most of us.

Imagine that you are attending an introductory workshop. You
join other students who are arriving and choosing their seats in the
circle. As the facilitator of the group, I am observing the differences

in their demeanor. Some seem excited and chatty, others reserved and quiet. There are those who've come with a friend and those who are clearly alone. One of them seems defensive, arms folded across his chest and a facial expression that seems to say, "I dare you to get me to open up." One woman arrives with a bunch of beautiful flowers and presents them to me with a smile that attempts to cloak the sadness in her eyes.

I begin the class by introducing myself and then asking each person to say their first name and why they're here. Most respond by saying something noncommittal, such as, "I heard about you from a friend," or "I'm into spiritual growth," or "I actually don't know why I'm here," or the one that always gets a laugh: "My wife made me come."

Then I ask what they believe their life's most challenging event or aspect to be. We go around the circle again, but this time the subject is more difficult. Most give it some sincere thought before answering, and some just blurt something out, embarrassing themselves, sometimes apologizing. Others say they can't think of anything. I encourage them by suggesting they close their eyes and imagine an event in their lives that they haven't been able to resolve and release, something that still causes pain or anger or confusion.

The answers intensify as each person in the circle shares, encouraging each successive person to share more deeply.

"I came from a very poor family. We all struggled to survive. Oh … and my mother died when I was eight."

"I just discovered that I have breast cancer, and I need some spiritual support. I'm very frightened!"

"We always had money—that was never the problem—and I'm pretty healthy. Uh, but I guess I'd say my challenge is that I've always felt alone. And stupid. They always told me I'd never amount to anything."

"I was sexually abused by my father from about two years old until I was a teen and moved out of the house."

"I was married for thirteen years to a man who beat me every time he got drunk—and that was on a daily basis. It ended when he died of a heart attack. I felt that was justice, since he'd broken my heart."

And the sharing continues. Suffering hearts, teary eyes, shaky voices, hope in their eyes. I know they are expecting me to take away their pain with a magic formula, some pop psychotherapy, a mystical ceremony, or a healing chant.

I sense what can trigger a deepening of their personal healing. So I say, "In a moment, I'm going to tell you something, and when I do, I want you to sense what your *immediate* feelings are about what I've just said."

I wait a moment for their nods of agreement. Some are hesitant, some enthusiastic.

I begin. "You are *not* a victim; there is *no such thing*. Instead, we all agree to create our realities, even when we're not consciously aware that we're doing so. As Souls, before each lifetime, we select joy or adversity, and the people who will abuse, mistreat, and hate us, as well as those who will support and love us. We do this for the purpose of our Souls' education and evolution. It can also be a loving agreement between ourselves and the Souls who will present challenges or support in our lives. They will agree to do this for us *because* they love us and want us to evolve."

I know this is hard to hear, maybe impossible to even consider, but as I say these things, I sense a huge energy shift in the room. I hear movement as some adjust their positions in their chairs. Someone coughs. I see a woman dabbing at her eyes with a tissue as someone else gets up and leaves. The man with the crossed arms seems less sure of himself. His eyes dart around the room as if to find an escape route, but he doesn't leave. *Good for him,* I think to myself.

This workshop consists of fictitious students but is representative of the feelings, attitudes, and hopes of so many whom I've worked with over the years. The concept of having agreed before birth to difficulties as well as successes in a lifetime is usually foreign to most and even unacceptable to others. But for those who can at least consider the idea of having made Soul choices and agreements before slipping into human lives, a whole new perspective of their perception of life emerges. And combined with the work in Separation, where we study how our thoughts create our reality, we can apply this to what we might choose between lives to create before birth into a new lifetime.

Imagine how you might feel if your therapist, counselor, minister, or wise friend told you that what you've always believed were your difficult, shameful, or undesirable traits and experiences were exactly what you *needed*—and perhaps, from a Soul standpoint, actually *chose*—to help you grow as a person and to evolve spiritually. (What are you feeling right now as you consider this possibly preposterous idea?) This is part of the work we do in Separation—being willing to look closely at everything we observe about ourselves, sorting it all out, and discovering how these things served us to become more conscious. But even more importantly, digging into them with a sincere intention to change our perceptions about whatever they present to us is the key to the next stage of alchemy, *Conjunction*. If these traits were specifically chosen by our Souls before we were born, it means that our work in transforming them gives the Soul the gift that emerges from the transformed trait. This could be something like doing Separation work on your inner critic and transforming it into your inner wisdom.

The concept of pre-birth choices and agreements between Souls can help us discover answers to existential questions such as, "Why was I born to this abusive family?" or "What is the purpose of my having a disability?" or "Why can't I succeed in my career or relationships?"

The 1991 film *Defending Your Life* portrays this concept of making life choices that support growth. In the film, the character played by Albert Brooks has died and is required in the afterlife to account for his life just lived. He is brought before a "court," whose purpose is not to judge him but to encourage him to see how he had judged himself as inferior and inadequate. In so doing, he hadn't lived his life to the fullest. His beliefs about himself were so impaired that he never risked doing what it would take to grow. Thanks to an evolved friend, played by Meryl Streep, he is inspired, through his attraction to her, to override his beliefs about his unworthiness and take a leap of faith into his next experience. In his earthly life he has been in hell, without even knowing it, and the Meryl Streep character becomes like Dante's Beatrice, leading him into the only thing that counts—love.

If, in my pre-birth state, I had chosen an "easy" and unconditionally loving family, I would never have needed to work as hard as I have on awakening to my greater consciousness. I could not trust my parents' ways of being with me because I had expected them to behave in ways they were unable to be. Consequently, my disappointment planted the seed that would grow and help me to trust myself. And because my parents found it difficult to accept me as an unusual and highly sensitive child, as well as not being their preferred boy child, I would need to find ways to accept myself. There was always something that I felt wasn't quite right with me, and for years I thought they had caused it. But I eventually realized that it was more like a switch within myself had been turned off by my Soul before birth so I would put every ounce of my attention and energy into learning how to turn it back on in a more evolved state.

A few years ago I flew to San Diego to visit my mother, whom I hadn't seen in some time. I had always dreaded visiting her because it brought up so much unresolved emotion within me, as well as disappointment that nothing had changed between us. Yet because I'd been working for some time on my projections onto her, I hoped that this trip might be different. (A projection is like a projector in a movie theater casting the film onto a screen. In human relationships, we project our unresolved issues onto others, blaming and making judgments—positive or negative. We project onto others what we don't want to see within ourselves. Most often, projections can be identified by their disproportionate reaction to the situation at hand.)

This time, I was surprised that we were both actually happy to see one another, although we still launched into the usual mindless conversation. I began to fear a re-ignition of the old "stuff" when suddenly, my mother's eyes began to sparkle and she stopped talking. She just looked at me, smiling.

I felt a rush of something arising within me and I burst out with, "You know, don't you? We're done, aren't we?"

Smiling more broadly, she just nodded.

In that amazing moment, we both knew that we had fulfilled our Souls' agreements with one another and were now free to celebrate the love between us that had been necessary to mask for so long. I could now appreciate what an amazing Soul she was and felt deep gratitude for her presence in my life. And, in a way, she released to me the gift of my identity, clearer than ever. I realized it had never been lost or stolen. It had been with me all along. But I had to discover it again by myself, not as a victim, but as an evolving Soul…and all the while she had been holding her knowledge of it in trust for me.

It wasn't until later that I began to understand what this was all about. Before we come into a lifetime, we must relinquish the memory of our existence between lives, or else we wouldn't feel motivated to grow. We'd already know who we were, where we had come from, and where we would go after the human life since we would also know that there is no death, that life is eternal. I had a dream once in which I am helping an old, wise woman prepare Souls for their trip to an earthly existence. The people are on a kind of conveyer belt, and she is teaching me how to perform what seems to me to be spiritual lobotomies. This is being done to make them forget their otherworldly lives so that they will be able to commit fully to their upcoming earthly ones.

Soul Choices Meditation

Relax in a comfortable position, eyes closed, and breathing easily and evenly. Do this for a few minutes to relax you further.

Now, without effort, allow some of your life's challenges to float across your mind. When one appears that you'd like to explore, become fully aware of the experience. The key here is not to sink back into the emotional triggers, but to observe the challenge as objectively as you can.

Now, imagine you and your Soul are in communication about this life issue. Ask your Soul why it chose to experience this particular challenge. Take the time you need to deeply listen to what your Soul tells you. Keep in mind that it may not speak to you in words—it may give you pictures or symbols.

Besides asking your Soul why it chose this issue, ask more questions, such as:

- What was it about the family you chose for me that was needed for our (your human aspect's and your Soul's) growth?
- How did (abuse, rejection, unreasonable expectations, restrictive parenting, limited opportunities, etc.) serve our growth?
- What would I not have learned had you chosen an entirely different type of family?
- What have we learned from the worst person in the family?
- Who ultimately turned out to be of great support to me, even if earlier he or she was not?
- How did I contribute to the problems within the family?
- Is it possible now for me to release my negative feelings and fears about certain family members? If so, when will I do this? How do I sense this will free me?

———◆———

Here is a simplified way to look at this idea of pre-birth Soul choices and how they affect our lives and evolvement. I'm going to break it down in stages, though please keep in mind that life doesn't follow formulas. I hope your imagination is stirred by this model.

1. In our life between lives, the Soul is led by its guides and teachers to make choices about parents, environment, and issues and challenges in the life to come. All these decisions are based upon what will enable the Soul to grow the most. There will also be agreements between Souls to assist each other in the upcoming life by being either each other's best friend or nemesis—again, all with the mission of helping both Souls to evolve. I believe most of these agreements are between deeply connected Soul friends who love each other enough to do

what they agree to for the sake of their beloved friend, even if their task seems difficult and painful.

2. The Soul is put through a process of forgetting its true self and its experiences between lives and during past lives. This is purposefully done so that there will be no distraction from the issues that have been agreed upon to face and learn to resolve. By forgetting who we truly are, we are motivated to learn new things, to push our growth beyond the known.

3. The Soul incarnates on Earth, and is shocked to enter the tiny body of a fetus in a womb.[5] Our original world appears very different in all ways from this dense, physical world. When going through the birth process, our little bodies experience pain as the uterus contracts. Lights on Earth are harsh, sounds grate on the sensitivities, we don't seem to fit in the infant body, gentle touch is both foreign and pleasurable, and if mishandled by a business-like doctor or unfeeling parent, the cells in our bodies hold this as a memory for life. No matter how traumatic, all of these experiences are part of the Soul's agreement to learn about its humanity in all its aspects, both delightful and painful, and to evolve as a result.

4. Having forgotten its agreement to learn from adversity, the Soul must struggle to decide whether to stay in this new, formidable experience on Earth. This is the time when infants may choose to die or continue on into a life. The trauma of this experience may be too much even with a strong agreement, and the Soul can always go back and try again at a more favorable time. Even if there is a shadow of memory about the agreement, it may seem so distant and impossible that the Soul chooses to re-enter its more familiar habitat. It is even possible that the Soul

---

5. Most Souls, according to the years of research done by Dr. Michael Newton, don't enter the physical body immediately, but usually wait until at least the fourth month or even the moment of birth. He says the older, wiser Souls enter earlier so they can prepare the mother's consciousness for the agreed-upon tasks. For a more detailed discussion, see Dr. Newton's *Destiny of Souls* (St. Paul, MN: Llewellyn Publications, 2000), 382–89.

only needed a few moments of experience in a human infant's body to gain what it needed and then can leave, purpose fulfilled. Sometimes the Soul's purpose in doing this is to assist the parents by presenting an opportunity to love in the face of tragedy. After one of my daughters had a miscarriage, I was doing energy work on her to help her heal physically and emotionally. Suddenly, I felt a huge presence behind me. Though I didn't see it with my physical eyes, I knew it was a being of light. Extrasensorily, it told me that it was the Soul who had come and left again for the purpose of its earthly parents' growth.

5. As the child grows, it begins to learn the things the Soul wanted it to come to Earth to discover: love, judgment, compassion, pain, suffering, joy, play, creative expression, and so much more. Even while the human aspect may not be aware, the Soul knows it is making progress.

6. The human may continue to suffer, but in so doing, it may offer great service to others, as the experience of suffering contributes to others' well-being and is an important offering to humanity.

7. The human self learns how to perceive differently by deep, inner, Soul-directed senses rather than by appearances. This is a result of the various alchemical stages, particularly Dissolution, which awakens our emotions.

8. The human aspect develops the ability to observe both outwardly and inwardly and learns ways to embody the results of those observations. This is the work we do in Separation, where we become more and more conscious of our inner and outer worlds as we deepen our observational skills.

9. Experience, coupled with compassion, leads the human aspect to eventually blend and harmonize with the Soul and its purpose. The human may experience wisdom, enlightened perceptions, and inner peace, knowing and sensing these things to be related to its eternal being. After experiencing the fine-tuning within *Putrefaction-Fermentation*, we move into the distilled state, where we are now able to rise above the level

of any problem. Author Robert Schwartz, an authority on between-lives experiences, writes: "Since we plan life's challenges to experience and know ourselves as love in all its many forms, then such challenges are rendered unnecessary if we arrive at that self-knowing before the challenge occurs."[6]

10. The human may reach self-awareness, where it realizes that all it has worked to gain and learn has been there all along, but it was merely fine-tuning to help the Soul aspect to evolve. Enlightenment isn't something it creates, it's something it remembers. It may also begin to recall more details of its origin. This is Coagulation—the gift of the Philosopher's Stone.

11. The human is now free to go back "home" when it chooses, or stay on Earth to help others grow as it has grown.

12. The Soul, when back in its between-lives realm, reviews what its human aspect helped it to learn. It then makes new decisions for the next experience, whether on a planetary plane or elsewhere in consciousness.

Our task is to consciously face and surrender to the lessons adversity can teach us. If not done consciously and willingly, suffering captures us, often by the painful deflation of the ego. Either way, we are initiated into the deeper mysteries of our authentic nature, signaling that it is ready to become more conscious. The demise of the ego's control and resultant integration of the Soul shocks us awake to expanded perceptions of being both spiritual *and* human. Investigative immersion into the underpinnings of belief leads to transformation of the belief, and this expands the underlying, original meaning of it.

As we climb out of the box of prohibitive, limited, and socially acceptable ways of being, we are freed to express things we never said but longed to say in support of ourselves and how we perceived the world. One of the best ways I know to do this is through the creative arts. By painting, making music, dancing, or writing poetry, we

6. Robert Schwartz, *Your Soul's Plan* (Berkeley, CA: Frog Books, 2009), 287.

plunge deeply into hidden resources within. This can lead us to cease resisting and begin to surrender to the will of the numinous. When we "give it up" to the Divine, we find it within.

Whenever I look back at how angry I used to be with my parents, from birth until well into my supposed "adulthood," I understand that I was like a petulant child who kept waiting for Mom and Dad to shape up and be the perfect parents I expected. Eventually, I tired of the pouty childishness within me—it just didn't fit any longer. I withdrew the projection of my issues onto my parents—even though they were the ones I'd agreed to before birth!—and started looking at what their behaviors mirrored in me. Whenever I felt rejected by them, my task was to determine how I was rejecting myself—or them—in the same way. Though this was painful and difficult, I was able to break away, a little more each time, from designing my life according to what my parents and others thought about me. Most importantly, I began to realize that others' criticisms and insensitivities to my sensitivities were mirrors of my own deep doubts about myself.

My attitude about my parents began to change. What I had always thought were my father's stern rules and criticisms of me actually assisted me in developing a strong determination to achieve my goals, especially when they didn't seem possible. His influence was what kept me going. As we both grew older, he would proudly refer to me as "feisty." The pressure he put on me in the early part of my life was a gift that would continue to make me stronger for the rest of my life. In a way, I think his disappointment that I wasn't a boy led him to push me in the same way he would have done if I *were* a son. I knew his urging me to succeed combined with my rebellion against it, and like a bowstring being pulled back tightly enough to shoot the arrow true, it created the tension that would help me learn to fly.

Two years before my father died, we had a conversation that surprised me. For the first time, this aeronautical engineer who helped design the space shuttle actually asked to hear about my work. He also shared with me something I could never have imagined. I told him I specialized in working with dreams. Suddenly, he bolted forward in his chair, eyes alight, and said, "Oh! I've had a dream over and over for years in which I am navigating a flying saucer by running my hands over crystals." I was knocked speechless. *My* father actually sharing something like this with me? And admitting to dreaming, which I had always assumed his technical mind would reject? And piloting flying saucers? I felt the walls between us crumbling. We had rediscovered the deeper Soul connection with each other that had been forgotten in our early years together in order to help each other grow.

I refer to Earth as "the workshop planet," since I sense its purpose is as a host habitat filled with opportunities, places both beautiful and treacherous, varieties of human cultures and societies, environmental richness, and powerful energies—all of which serve us in our growth. Each lifetime holds critically important lessons that our Souls need. When we go through what I called earlier our "spiritual lobotomy," this memory devolution helps us fully face our earthly challenges and be strengthened and accelerated by them until such time as we are ready to accept an even greater level of awareness of our Divinity.

Recently, a student came excitedly into class, tears glistening in her eyes. She grasped my hands and thanked me for having presented these ideas the week before. She had always had a contentious relationship with her mother and couldn't understand why it was so difficult—that is, until she adopted the concept of having made pre-birth Soul agreements with her mother. She was now able to release her concretized beliefs about her mother. She told me that her perceptions of the relationship felt very different. She now saw her mother as having given her important gifts. They were now able to be with one another without the old tension, and they had begun actually enjoying their time together.

When goldsmiths work with gold, they add other precious metals in order to strengthen it. When we are faced with adverse challenges by a significant person in our lives, like my student's mother, they are like the strengthening metals that reinforce our inner gold so we can begin to recognize its radiance.

As we move into the next stage, *Conjunction*, we use what we have learned in Separation and bring it all back together again. This may sound strange, but everything we transformed in Separation by learning of its opposites must be rejoined, but this time in a balanced way—As above, so below. Remember, one of the rules of the alchemical transformative process is that we can't get rid of anything. We can only change its relationship to us by our thinking and creation of new beliefs. In the next chapter, we'll explore more about this sacred marriage of opposites.

SUMMARY POINTS

- In Separation, we gain aspects of ourselves we may never have been aware of before.

- The alchemical maxim "As above, so below" means we connect to and blend the earthly and the heavenly within us when we do the work of alchemical transformation. It tells us that whatever is done in the higher realms of consciousness can be brought to the lower, earthly realm, and vice versa. It is a sacred marriage of states of consciousness.

- The key to dealing with challenge and adversity is to discover ways to transform our perceptions of these experiences. We need to find how the situation serves us—then we transform it and we grow from this transition.

- Understanding pre-birth choices and agreements with other Souls helps us know why we've had to experience certain things in our human lifetime. By doing this, we release thinking of ourselves as innocent victims and begin believing ourselves to be courageous seekers of Soul growth.

- As we grow, we can begin to see things about our families that we couldn't before while we were trying to protect ourselves. We can now see how the members of our families were gifts to us to help us grow.

- In alchemical transformation, we can't get rid of anything—we can only change its relationship to us by our thinking and creation of new beliefs.

CHAPTER 7

CONJUNCTION

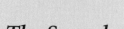

The Sacred Marriage

"Continued enlightenment comes from living within the Operation of the Sun."
~ALCHEMICAL ARCANUM FOUR

The alchemical arcanum for *Conjunction* tells us that in order to grow spiritually, we must look to higher sources than those within ordinary consciousness. It uses the metaphor of the interrelationship between our planet Earth as our Mother and the Sun as our Father, both givers of life but in different ways. The relationship between the two are a marriage of opposite energies that are dependent upon one another. As we work to integrate and balance our human equivalents to these universal masculine and feminine forces, our hearts are opened. With an open heart, we can deal with challenges from a consciousness of love, rather than self-protection and resistance.

According to Dennis Hauck, the purpose of the fourth stage of alchemical transformation, Conjunction, is "…the creation of a unified self that is true to both inner essences and universal truths and can withstand the onslaughts of ignorance, insensitivity, and illusion one encounters in the world. Conjunction gives us the equanimity necessary to carry on with the higher operations of Alchemy."[7]

The higher alchemical operations involve a blending and unification of both masculine and feminine traits that are aspects within us all. In the stage of Conjunction, this work of balancing and bringing these two aspects together in a Sacred Marriage must continue to progress in each following stage until Coagulation, where they have completely conjoined in a consciousness of heart-based wholeness.

Brugh Joy, MD, my spiritual teacher for over thirty years, taught that nothing is more important than heart-centered awareness. He developed his teaching based upon what he saw as the four attributes of the heart: compassion, innate harmony, the healing presence, and unconditional love. Alchemical Conjunction opens the heart to these attributes after the transformations in the three previous stages, and creates a grounded foundation for the next stages.

---

7. Dennis William Hauck, *The Emerald Tablet* (New York: Penguin, 2009), 215.

Alchemy's principle "As above, so below" means that Earth and Heaven are interwoven, inseparable. What happens in the earthly field also occurs in the higher realms, and vice versa. Alchemists seek the balance between the two realms, and from that balance comes transformation, healing, and change. Conjunction is like the archetypal image of the World Tree, where the spiritual meets the physical. This symbol, found in many mystical traditions—such as Yggdrasil in Norse mythology, the mystical Judaic Kabbalah, the trees of life and knowledge in Genesis, and the Tree of Souls in the film *Avatar*—illustrates that wholeness results from stretching our "branches" to the heavens, sinking our roots deeply in the earth, and maintaining our trunk as a highway that flows between the two realities.

Just as entering into a marriage requires serious thought and dedication to love and service in partnership, Conjunction requires deep surrender and a willingness to release the ego's obsolete protections. Just as in a true marriage, we are no longer one person with our own likes, dislikes, and ways of being. Rather, in conjoined consciousness, we blend with another, deeper, higher consciousness with a result of selflessness. Whether in a mature and fulfilling marriage or within our inner work with ourselves, we grow and become more of ourselves while melding with our partner or inner aspects until there is no separation. This is unified consciousness.

Here is a meditation to help you gain insight into how opposites— in this case, the feminine and masculine—must work in communion with one another to affect a consciousness of wholeness. This requires *inclusion* rather than rejection and furthers the transformation of the ego-protector's limiting "either/or" position, which insists that one idea or choice is preferable over the other. Conversely, the conjuncted person is able to see each opposite as balance for the other. Without the night and with only the day, or vice versa, all life on Earth would be severely imbalanced. Thus it is with other pairs, such as dark and light, up and down, left and right, right and wrong, and feminine and masculine aspects.

CONJUNCTION MEDITATION

Sit in a comfortable posture and close your eyes, perhaps with quiet music playing. Imagine yourself in a serene place in nature. You are sitting quietly on a bench or log when you become aware of a man and woman slowly approaching from the distance. As they move toward you, be aware of how they appear physically—how they look, what they are wearing, etc. As they move closer to you, use your intuition and body sense to discern your feelings about both of them. What are you sensing about their intention, attitude, or beingness?

Now begin to notice how they interact with one another. Listen to how they converse, how they react or respond.

Now they approach you. Ask them to introduce themselves to you and listen for their names or perhaps descriptive words they share. Ask them what they have to tell you about themselves. This is a most important part of this meditation, so take the time you need to listen without editing what they do or say. You'll soon discover how meaningful this conversation will be for you. Ask them what their needs are and if those needs are being fulfilled, how they want to express themselves, and what they want you to know about them and the purpose and dynamics of their relationship.

When you feel they have given you all they can for this time, thank them and conclude your meditation. Write down what you learned about these two, who are your inner masculine and feminine, how they relate to one another, and how they affect your life.

———◆———

The attributes of the heart that are developed in Conjunction create new perceptions of how we feel about ourselves and others. If we have been afraid to love unconditionally, restore harmony, lend our healing presence, or show compassion, the heart stays closed and confirms our belief that we are victims, unlovable and unworthy. Most of the world's religions teach that forgiveness is the key to the heart. But some believe these teachings imply that forgiveness requires self-negation, which I see as being very different from selflessness. I don't believe that is what true forgiveness is. If we wish to stop blaming others and forgive them, we must embody a new level of compassion that is based upon acceptance and understanding. Rather than trying to forgive because we feel anxious and guilty, which inhibits true forgiveness, our intention must be to understand and accept others' roles in our lives unconditionally, sensing that we may have made Soul agreements that are affecting us now.

This is exceptionally difficult to do when dealing with someone with whom our Soul has made an agreement involving some sort of unthinkable trauma or abuse. It is a formidable task to understand why we may have chosen to suffer at the hands of another. When we can finally release into understanding and compassion, forgiveness radically shifts from being a half-hearted pardon of someone who has harmed us to profound gratitude for how they helped us grow.

The battles we have within ourselves about having been harmed by another can be either short-lived and productive, or long-lasting and life-exterminating. Many of us lug a weighty container around with us, loading it over and over with things we are afraid to face directly. We believe we have been harmed by others, and are unwilling to look at what the situation is trying to teach us. We have a choice to make: we can continue to hold on to our heavy beliefs or let them go, freeing ourselves as well as those we resent and fear. A choice to hold on to the past is like an alchemist who refuses to proceed with the next laboratory process—his choice would guarantee that he would never conjure gold.

This is a formidable concept to grasp when blame, anger, resentment, and grief hold us firmly in a consciousness of negative beliefs. We are trapped in a prison of self-condemnation until we are willing to let go and acknowledge *gratitude* for the lessons we are given. When we hold fiercely to old beliefs, we create our own suffering, which continues until we decide to change our attitude toward the old beliefs.

You may recoil from this concept and ask: "How can I be grateful for a husband who beats me?" "What's so positive about my cancer?" "Why should I thank my parents for abandoning me?" "Are you saying we should be doormats?" Of course not! But it's essential to consider abuses and challenges without denial, blame, or the impulse to sugarcoat, which only serves to perpetuate pain and mask the real purpose. This task requires that we must first release the pattern of feeling sorry for ourselves, which is built upon the idea that suffering is a punishment for being less than we were meant to be. By freeing our belief in this pattern, we redeem the gift in the experience rather than reengaging the trauma.

In the Arthurian tale of Parsival, King Arthur trains and protects the young knight until such time as the kingdom falls into dire chaos. Arthur sends out his strongest knights to find the mystical grail that legends say can save the realm. However, when they all return empty-handed and despairing, Arthur has no choice but to send the young and inexperienced Parsival in search of it.

The grail may not have been anything physical, such as a chalice, but it is a rather apt symbol of the value of the gold within us. In this story, after employing all of his masculine resources to no avail and almost giving up by believing himself to be a victim of fate, Parsival finally gains the grail by surrendering to his feminine, caring, sensitive nature—he opens his heart to authentic love.

Youthful Parsival is delighted to have been chosen and is unwavering in his belief that it will be he who retrieves the holy icon. He sets out one fine morning on his trusty steed, loping along, enjoying the ride. He estimates that finding the precious cup will take him about a day.

Weeks later, exhausted, confused, and lost, Parsival and his horse are dragging slowly and dejectedly along the road when he spots a castle on the horizon. He is greatly relieved to see that it's one he hasn't visited yet and that he hasn't just been going around in circles.

He rides up to the drawbridge, sitting straight and strong in his saddle, then proudly demands entry, and leaves his horse with a groom. He is told that he is awaited in the Great Hall by the king of this realm.

Parsival enters the hall and is dazzled by its beauty and majesty. The steward seats him at a lavishly spread table next to the king, who is lying on his side on a bench at the table. Parsival wonders at this but avoids looking at the ruler. Had he looked, he would have seen a large, gaping wound in the king's leg. At this point in his young life, self-conscious Parsival doesn't know what to do for the king, so he avoids the issue by enjoying himself too much to get involved.

Parsival digs into his food, enjoying the minstrel's songs and the piper's music. His attention is drawn to a doorway, where he sees a procession of seven beautiful princesses entering the Great Hall. The first princess carries a silver tray, upon which stands the grail in all its glory. Parsival's mouth drops open with disbelief that it will be so easy to take the cup back to Arthur.

Before he has a chance to close his gaping mouth, the entire castle and its jugglers and musicians, king and princesses alike, dissolve before his eyes. He stares, shocked, in disbelief. He leaps up, whipping his head from side to side, in an attempt to bring back the now non-existent castle. He falls to the ground on his knees, not believing how his luck has betrayed him, and drops his head, weeping with grief and frustration. He believes fate has intervened because he is not worthy, but he doesn't know why.

After some time, his horse gently nudges him, and Parsival arises, agonizing over his ill fortune. Aching with sorrow, he pulls himself onto his horse's back and slowly rides away, knowing he must continue his search, since giving up and going back to Arthur without the grail would mean sure death for them all.

Years pass. Slumped over on his decrepit horse, Parsival is now a very old man, worn out, weak, and ill of heart, with tears falling down his face in an unending stream. He rarely stops to drink from the brooks or take food from local farmers. Each day he thinks this will be his last moment on Earth.

Suddenly something draws his attention. As he pulls his head up, his rheumy eyes see—or believe they see—the same castle he'd seen so many years before. He squeezes his eyes shut, rubs them, and opens them again, disbelieving that he could possibly have traveled in such a great circle for so long.

He found the grail to be an illusion the last time around, so he feels no hope in finding it again. Nevertheless, he walks his horse onto the drawbridge, surrenders the animal to the groom, and limps into the Great Hall.

He is amazed at what he sees. The hall is filled with the same beauty, the same entertainers, the same princesses, and the same king after all these years. He is convinced he is dreaming.

Sure that this must be the day of his death, he sits down next to the king, who is once again lying on the bench. This time, however, having matured and been tossed about by "fate," Parsival looks at him directly, then down at the festering leg. He addresses the king directly.

"Sire, what ails thee?"

At this, the king rises to a sitting position, his leg instantly healed by Parsival's sincere compassion. Parsival feels a sense that he's been freed of his old beliefs that had prevented his obtaining the grail. His compassion has healed him as well as the king. Looking Parsival in the eye and smiling, the king then motions toward the doorway, where the seven princesses emerge. Again, the first princess carries the grail in on a silver tray.

Parsival turns to the king and asks, deeply, from his heart, "How does the grail serve?"

In a flash, Parsival realizes that the spiritual secret of the grail lies in the acceptance of the power of love and compassion. He finds himself young again as the castle disappears once more. He rides his revitalized horse into Arthur's castle, holding the grail high in the air. Sir Parsival presents it to his king, and the castle magically transforms into its original beauty and majesty. The grail, as the embodiment of the feminine, restores balance to the ailing masculine realm, and Arthur's kingdom is reborn, no longer preyed upon by their fears.

In Shakespeare's *King Lear*, the old king refuses over and over to release his fear-based control. Finally, beaten down, penniless, and wandering with only a young servant, Lear finally inquires as to the young man's comfort, just as Parsival finally asks the king what ails him. The move from self-obsession to compassion is a powerful key in transformation.

These stories demonstrate how, when choosing to follow the stereotypical masculine path exclusively (note that I say *stereotypical* masculine path—I'm not referring to the true masculine, which carries strength, fortitude, honor, respect, innovation, intelligence, and more), we fool ourselves with fear-based bravado and false, narrow-minded beliefs. The resolution lies in surrendering to what has been missing: the feminine within both women and men. A contentious and competitive relationship limits us to a horizontal experience, rather than an ascension into higher realms of consciousness. In the conjoining of the masculine with the feminine in the *hieros gamos*, the Sacred Marriage, the ego relinquishes its role as the prime director and a mutually harmonious relationship emerges.

It takes Parsival many years to make the profound shift from self-obsessed perceptions to compassionate service. Even if we consider that time and space are only relative to the human mind, we have chosen to be human for a while, so these Divine processes take time. We must experience repeatedly, as did Parsival, whatever we most need to learn until we are ready to embody it.

Imagine a spiral shape—like an ice cream cone standing upright—made of wire that winds around, widening at the top as it increases in height. Next, picture a straight, golden rod that is attached to the side of the spiral from bottom to top of the wire cone. See how it touches each turn of the wire as it comes around again.

The spiral symbolizes how we heighten and increase the breadth of our spiritual evolvement. It depicts how, each time a challenge, represented by the golden rod, is triggered, it occurs on a more expansive level of awareness, because we've progressed since the last time the event happened in our life. This increases our awareness so we can perceive it differently and with more wisdom each time we encounter it. Eventually the golden rod that represents the challenge merges with the energy of the spiral itself as a lesson fully learned and integrated.

The mother of a student of mine committed suicide by hanging herself. My student was the one who found her and was understandably shocked, but proceeded to take on the responsibility of all the preparations for burial. The trauma of finding her mother dead numbed her at first, but as she and I worked on her feelings about it over time, it became clear that she was afraid to face the reality of what had happened. She had a wonderful intellect but used it to "think away" her feelings, so she had not truly grieved her loss. She feared that if she dove into what had happened, she'd be overwhelmed with uncontrollable pain, from which she'd be permanently scarred. I could not give her any guarantee of what might happen, but when I described the idea of the spiral that I just mentioned, she was able to accept that her healing would take time. This helped her take her process out of her intellect and put it into the feelings that were waiting to be expressed. She could relate to the golden rod, which gave her ease in her process of grieving. This empowered her to move on from the shock and pain of her mother's suicide and out of the hiding place in her intellect. She became willing to leap into the fire of Calcination to explore her ego-protector that had encouraged her to intellectualize her mother's death rather than feel it.

The most important key to the work we did together was when she was able to release her anger at the way her mother died. She had held her anger as a shield against what she imagined her mother's purpose had been in committing suicide. When she was able to see her mother as having hidden her emotional agony that led to her death, she was able to see the way she, herself, had always closeted her emotions in favor of her intellect. She was now able to see a similarity in their emotional makeup, and was able to understand more about the death but mainly about the value of her own emotions. For her, this was a Conjunction experience because she was able to recognize her mother's resistance to showing feelings and bring this realization together with her own new view of the gold within her.

In the first three stages of alchemical transformation, we learn what has caused suffering in our lives: low self-esteem, fear of feeling emotions, not feeling equal to others, being afraid to express creatively, hiding behind our intellect, or covering fears about ourselves by working nonstop. The stage of Conjunction continues to break free the old beliefs and behaviors, and bring in a new consciousness that teaches us ways to deal with adversity with an open heart. By replacing who we always thought we were with new perceptions that are uncovered in the process of Conjunction, we become more conscious of the marriage of Soul and Spirit within us and we become more authentic, more whole, and closer to our golden core. We learn to walk in balance on the earth at the same time we feel our integration with the heavens.

Summary Points

- Within the fourth stage of alchemical transformation, Conjunction, the higher aspects of opposites blend together to create the balance and strength we need for the higher stages of the work.

- This stage teaches the equal value of both heavenly and earthly experience.

- Grounding in the heart in a balance of Heaven and Earth means embracing the four attributes of heart-level consciousness as taught by Brugh Joy: compassion, innate harmony, the healing presence, and unconditional love.

- The alchemical integrative principle of "As above, so below" means that Earth and Heaven are interwoven—what happens in either affects both.

- Unified consciousness is created by a conjunction between any pair of opposites, so there is no separation between them. It requires inclusion rather than exclusion or rejection.

- True forgiveness comes from understanding and acceptance of the purpose of the other person's role in your life. It may be a Soul agreement made pre-birth between the two of you, so forgiveness and gratitude to the person for having helped you grow results.

- A choice to hold on to the past is like an alchemist who refuses to proceed with the next laboratory process—his choice would guarantee that he would never conjure gold.

- The task of forgiveness begins with stopping the pattern of feeling sorry for oneself; only then can it move on to understanding ourselves or another person through compassion and selflessness.

- In the Parsival tale, the two most important teachings are the questions "What ails thee?" and "How does this serve?" When we ask ourselves these questions and answer honestly, we can understand the purpose of whatever challenge we are going through.

CHAPTER 8

THE GIFT IN ADVERSITY

You Have More Power Than You Think

One of the many pre-life choices our Souls may make with an intention of growth through adversity is to agree to come into a lifetime with deep feelings of inadequacy. That was certainly true in my case. Many of us suffer this challenge of low self-esteem and negative self-image for the purpose of learning how to accept all our aspects, whether easy or difficult, pleasing or unpleasant, unconditionally. Our choice offers us the gift of self-realization and conscious awakening. When we grow into unconditional self-acceptance, we remember our Soul's purpose on Earth as well as our unique spiritual identity—this is the alchemical maxim "As above, so below." In transforming our perceptions and attitudes of ourselves from fragmented to whole, from negative to positive, we unify with the true purpose of our being. You will find a way to discover this in Appendix A: The Gold Within You Process.

For some of us, low self-esteem is compensated for by ego inflation. It's like a balloon being blown up, and as it grows larger it pushes everything else out of the way until we no longer consciously pay attention to the underlying issue of self-worth. It is still there, however, and we experience a variety of conscious and subconscious feelings about our worth. We can chose to ignore them or project them onto others.

In my own case, to compensate for my lack of self-confidence, my ego inflated and created an overshadowing personality of arrogance, snobbishness, haughtiness, and a strong projected belief that I was better than others, as if I were royalty. This masked my deepest pain, but I still experienced feeling lost and alone. I vacillated between despair and arrogance, which was how the ego protected me from my pain. But this was never totally successful in disguising the fact that I was actually very scared inside.

Not everyone's ego employs inflation to hide negative beliefs, yet the ego always strives to compensate for difficult feelings and beliefs. When we believe ourselves to be inadequate in any way, our egos develop some kind of protective behavior or role to cover the unacceptable parts of ourselves—even our positive, powerful aspects that we can't quite believe. An example of another protective role the ego gives us is the "good girl" or "good boy," who practices placing themselves last, appearing to be selfless when actually the mask of sweetness and light covers desperation, disdain for oneself, powerlessness, and depression. Challenged self-esteem may also be submerged under rageful behavior, taking offense, intellectualizing, overspending ("retail therapy"), misuse of substances (drugs, alcohol, food, etc.), inappropriate humor, greed, sexual addiction, or ruthlessness and workaholism.

I've counseled many people who have a deeply rooted belief in their own inadequacy. These are primarily women, though low self-regard is genderless. Low self-esteem is epidemic in our society, though its origins can be found in periods of history that influenced the collective psyche in repressive and restrictive ways, such as the moral codes of the Victorian age. This epidemic has grown exponentially due to the barrage of commercial, religious, and social pressures in our culture to maintain certain acceptable behaviors, appearances, and performances that distance us from our authenticity. We are expected to run as fast as we can to keep up with this false code of getting by in the world. We frantically race to get ahead of everyone else while secretly believing, thanks to television commercials and celebrity influences, that we aren't thin enough, pretty enough, rich enough, or "cool" enough. Underlying all of our frantic efforts to be someone other than ourselves is the belief that *we* aren't enough.

Many suffer this fragmentation of self. We view ourselves as a container of rejectable parts. This fragmentation creates leaks in our energy fields, which invite others' negative energies into our fields like a magnet. The wheel of self-negation is reinforced as more negativity is added to it. We attempt to escape it but eventually succumb to the gravity of the wheel's perpetual motion. We reach out to others for security, trying to pull them in, and finally realize it doesn't work because our energy continues leaking, fragmenting us even more, and adding to our insecurities. It's not the absence or presence of others that creates security;

it's the presence of self solidly secured in our energy field. This sense of security can only be realized by transforming the habit of judging ourselves and developing the gift of seeing direction and higher purpose in adversity.

As we develop spiritually and step out of the box of convention, we begin to suspect that the choice our Souls made to suffer feelings of inadequacy was about learning to respond to our true needs, gifts, and purpose. We learn that outer experience is merely there to mirror back to us what is going on *within* ourselves.

Here's an exercise to help you become more aware of the habits that block you from honestly and unconditionally accepting yourself so you can experience the alchemical stage of Distillation. It takes time to become consciously aware of our habits, and this exercise is very effective if you take the time to keep the records on a daily basis for at least one month.

SELF-ACCEPTANCE EXERCISE

Make a list of how you disconnect from yourself because of fear. Items on your list might be eating, watching TV, overwork, using alcohol or recreational drugs, overspending, and worry. Each time you catch yourself in one of these activities, stop, breathe, pull yourself back inside yourself, and observe, *without judgment,* what *feelings* are present. An essential key in this exercise is the understanding that it's not the fear that wounds or heals, it's how you reject or accept your emotions.

A good practice is to keep a small notebook in which you make daily entries. Record the date, enter any of the habits that keep you from facing yourself, and then each time you observe yourself involved in one of these habits, just put a little check mark by it. At the end of the day look back at how many marks you have next to each item. The point of this exercise is to observe how your *judgment* might be coloring the reporting of the habits. If your self-criticism is strong enough, it may prevent you from even writing anything down. It might lead you to believe that looking at all the check marks might make you feel like a failure. But be very cautious of this trick of the ego-protector. If you keep this diary for at least a week (a month is preferable), you'll learn much about how you subconsciously berate yourself and how you can transform it through unconditional observation. Remember what the quantum physicists learned: whatever is observed changes.

⫸◆⫷

At a time in my life when I was struggling with my issue of inadequacy and ego inflation, I had a dream that I wasn't able to appreciate fully until many years later. This is one of the most important reasons to keep a journal of dated dreams: so we can look back and see how our dreams foretell events in our lives and spiritual development. In most dreams, all characters and aspects are parts of ourselves, so this particular dream's full meaning eluded me because the feelings of inadequacy or compensatory arrogance would have led me to believe that I was either a great guru or that the dream couldn't possibly relate to me.

In this dream, I am in a foreign country with the guru Swami Muktananda, known as Baba to his devotees. The location is a lush, green area surrounding a lovely, circular lake, where lesser gurus and their families live in various parts around the lake. Everything is brightly colored and there are flowers in abundance. Everyone is wearing saris and breechcloths in vivid colors. I am both observer and participant and I am mated to one of the lesser gurus, who begins to exhibit symptoms of a fatal disease. Gifts are fashioned for him as part of a death ritual. I am creating a sort of kaleidoscope for him so that he can watch each color as it combines with others to form new colors.

I look over to his hut, where he sits cross-legged with his eyes rolled up. He falls backward onto some pillows and I think he has died. Baba calls him back to consciousness and writes on a small chalkboard the reasons why his healing will take place. I am not able to see what he writes.

When my mate awakens fully, his disease has been healed. A celebration ritual begins, with lovely women swimming underwater in the lake and then emerging, carrying gifts for him. I am moved by the beauty of the women and by their sincere devotion. Their faces glow as they come up out of the water and offer the gifts. They give them to the guru, who hands the gifts to me, and I put them in a stack for my healed partner.

The dream announced a readiness within me to heal the breach between my inner feminine and masculine aspects—to move into Conjunction—and that I was receiving spiritual help to do so. Because my ego inflation had put so much energy into defending me, the healing-integration process required the full participation of my masculine, who had been weakened through not being recognized or used, to begin the healing process. The masculine had to be healed by a change of perception about what the masculine truly is. My ego-protector tried to convince me that I could do everything myself and didn't need any help. My inadequacy aspect feared the masculine because I'd taken on society's stereotypical definition of it as a rough, unpredictable, overpowering force that I wanted nothing to do with. So the dream encouraged me to blend my feminine aspects with the masculine, which had suffered that stereotype long enough. It had made him ill. It was up to me to heal him through my ability to envision the highest potentials. The kaleidoscope's bright and varied colors symbolized a new way of perceiving the relationship between my inner masculine and feminine, as well as adding new frequencies, through the colors, that would heal me.

At the time I had this dream, I felt wonderful upon waking and for a few days afterward. But because my sense of self was not yet sturdy enough to fully embody the dream's message, I came crashing down. To successfully transform an issue that carries a great amount of energy, the shift in consciousness must equal or surpass the energy of the original issue. For me, the shift was to occur slowly over many years' time, alchemically transforming me as I matured emotionally and spiritually. I began to learn that my ego's choice of arrogance and haughtiness as buffers for my feelings of inadequacy hid within them a power that would take time to uncover. The ego had been misusing this power in order to protect me when I was unable to protect myself. What was hidden deep within me was the power of my Soul. With the eventual transformation of the compensatory haughty aspects of self, I was able to understand how my Soul was my authentic foundation, and very much a part of the gold within me.

Ancient Egyptian cosmology taught that there are several aspects to the Soul, one of which they called the *Sheut,* or shadow. They believed that the Sheut was always present within the individual, and neither could exist without the other. The Egyptians also believed that the shadow contained aspects of the person that were integral to survival. When combined with other Egyptian spiritual beliefs—such as their deep beliefs about the importance of death and the afterlife, the honoring and balancing of the feminine and masculine, and the integration of their spiritual beliefs in every aspect of their daily lives—it would follow that their idea of the shadow would mean something far more accepted and integrated than we now allow. Their Sheut would be more an ally than an adversary.

The shadow played an important part in an experience I had a few years ago. I felt that I had failed in my role as director of EarthSpirit Center. Some of my original students and board of advisors had left. But I was unable to see how my ego-controller, particularly the stereotypical masculine aspect of it, had disempowered people from fully expressing themselves because it had to be "my way." I didn't see how that turned people off, pushed them away, and disappointed them. Enrollment in my classes and counseling appointments began to drop as well, and I was in great emotional pain. I believed my vanishing students and what appeared to be the dissolution of EarthSpirit confirmed my negative beliefs about myself.

I was at a loss about what to do, because my ego was still in charge. I feared that if I couldn't rule my domain, it meant I had failed. My ego left little space for anything other than this concept. If I couldn't do what I'd been doing for so many years, what would I do? How would I make a living? How would I support myself? In all my mental, fear-based machinations, I was forgetting one of Brugh's teachings:

"Rise above the level of the problem." Even Einstein knew this, yet the truth of it still eluded me because I wasn't practicing it.

Unbeknownst to me at the time, the answer would emerge in a strong pull toward Northern California, specifically to a small Gold Rush–era community that I found to be healing and inspirational. While I felt terrified that my life as I knew it was dying, I spent time getting to know this little community, making new friends and eventually moving there. My rational mind wondered, if I couldn't make a living in the huge metropolis of Los Angeles, how could I possibly survive in a place with only 15,000 people? Nevertheless, I knew I had to live in this special place. Moving there meant I would have to face leaving my two daughters and their families in Southern California, including my beloved grandchildren, seven hours away. For three months I grieved the loss. I cried. I tried to think my way out of it, yet it became increasingly clear that I must leave Los Angeles. My Soul was in charge now, and it said, "Get moving!"

So I proceeded to leave Los Angeles, still grieving about my family. But I had a yard sale, packed up my belongings, and prepared for my new life. After releasing my family and accessing my courage to do this by myself, my older daughter suddenly announced that she and her family would also be moving to Northern California! I was stunned by this turn of events. It clearly confirmed that my letting go and trusting my inner guidance allowed everything else to find its right action.

When doing any sort of self-development work, it is essential to consider that *nothing* about us is inherently bad or wrong. Even within my compensatory ego-protector role, I found truth. People of royal birth may be haughty, but they are people just like the rest of us, so their arrogance is most likely a defense mechanism, just as mine was. However, attributes of true nobility—such as integrity, honor, gentility, morality, virtue, and service to others—are difficult to embody if we believe they couldn't possibly be true about us. When I followed my inner guidance to make a move in my life, my perception of work changed from that of making a living to that of heart-based service. I no longer concerned myself with whether or not my students would like me or would continue attending classes. Effort was no longer required. I allowed myself to simply enjoy the growth of my students and my own growth along *with* them.

The old adage "Whatever doesn't kill you makes you stronger" describes how adversity is the grist for the mill of our consciousness. In the midst of challenging conditions, most of us don't see the rewards. But with the courage to believe in yourself, and trusting the process, you will eventually understand how the difficult choices you made before you were born hold powerful gifts within them that will blossom into experiences of your true being. Overriding adversity with belief in yourself can produce miracles!

Summary Points

- One of the pre-birth challenges some of us choose is low self-esteem, or feelings of inadequacy. The purpose of this choice is to learn to accept all our aspects, no matter how easy or difficult.

- As we grow into unconditional self-acceptance, we begin to recall our Soul's purpose in choosing this challenge as well as our Soul's main purpose in who we are to become.

- Low self-esteem is often compensated for by ego inflation—we ignore our authentic feelings and needs, and the ego protects them through various inflated beliefs and attitudes.

- Society contributes to low self-regard through commercial, religious, and social pressures whose purpose is to maintain acceptability.

- Belief in our inadequacy fragments us, and we can't keep up with all the many aspects within us. This causes loss of energy, so we are vulnerable to outside negative influences.

- Security does not come from outside ourselves—it's the solid presence of our true self that creates feelings of security.

- Dreams can show us where we are in our growth process. In most dreams, all the characters and aspects are parts of ourselves to teach us what is happening in our consciousness.

- When we have transformational experiences that we are not quite ready for, it can cause negative feelings of failure, depression, or disbelief in the experience. Many times this "crash" is caused by the ego trying to protect us from growth.

- Our shadow aspect is essential to pay attention to because it not only holds difficult feelings we have tried to ignore, it also holds many of our gifts and talents that we have been afraid to bring to manifestation.

- An important key in transformational work is to know that nothing about us is inherently bad or wrong, even when the ego tries to convince us of our unworthiness in its attempt to continue controlling us.

- Adversity is the grist for the mill of consciousness work. It grinds away the old outdated beliefs by challenging them. This battle is difficult but if faced with a knowledge that something is wanting to change within us, we will come to see the rewards.

CHAPTER 9

PUTREFACTION-FERMENTATION

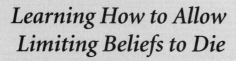

Learning How to Allow
Limiting Beliefs to Die

"The gateway to the Above
is through the True Imagination."
~ALCHEMICAL ARCANUM FIVE

The *Putrefaction-Fermentation* stage of transformational alchemy deepens the work done in Calcination, where fire incinerated material within the ego that limits, controls, and is no longer needed, as well as the three stages of Dissolution, Separation, and Conjunction. This time there is a fire of greater intensity that integrates lower levels of consciousness with the higher through fire and ferment. This work takes place in the higher realms of consciousness within us as well as universally in the collective unconscious.

Though Putrefaction can be a very disturbing experience, because it requires facing our darker aspects, we sense an ineffable change in progress. Some people in this stage report the ability to observe objectively even while experiencing deep and difficult feelings. The lower, ego-driven aspect of self is beginning to separate and make space for what wants to come forth as authentic guidance and wisdom. It is much like the booster rockets that separate from the space shuttle when they are no longer needed because the shuttle has attained the speed required to fulfill its goal.

This stage of Putrefaction shows us how aspects within us, even after Conjunction, still fight for dominance. The good news is that Fermentation, though still a formidable work, settles this process down as the dead or dying, putrefying aspects of us start to fertilize the seeds of growth.

Putrefaction is the process of decomposition before Fermentation can take place. It means that we have to *decompose* or *deconstruct* ourselves before we can completely conjoin with Soul. When we are "cooked" enough in this cauldron of *disintegration*, we enter Fermentation. This is similar to how grapes become wine or what happens to caterpillars when they create their cocoons. While inside, waiting to become butterflies, they disintegrate and become a jelly-like mush. Imagine a gorgeous butterfly transforming from that!

Putrefaction-Fermentation winnows our relationship to ego, separating out the unneeded so that it can now support rather than sabotage. Old beliefs, attitudes, and habits are broken down in the fiery soup. When an alchemist works with putrefied material, the brew must be transferred to another container to await the fermentation process. This is a metaphor for the newly developing self, having been separated from the old and being prepared for the new.

At this point in alchemical transformation, as well as in winemaking, a catalyst is added to produce the final stages of Fermentation. Our personal catalyst may be a trauma or profound loss or disappointment where we question our strongly held beliefs. This catalyst combines with what has been *decomposed* and a new identity is *composed*. Depression, disturbing dreams, and a deep need to be alone often signal this process. The task is in *allowing* the process to work on us rather than avoiding, rejecting, or denying it.

Putrefaction-Fermentation offers an opportunity to be led through our inner darkness to previously unknown parts of self. It disconnects us from the past, allowing it to die, rot, and ferment, providing the compost for the growth away from fear. We sit in the midst of bleak, dark, despairing emotions, being willing to not chase them away or misinterpret their presence. This is clearly not a time to "make nice" or pull prematurely out of our wretched state, but to just *be* with it so we develop the trust and wisdom toward which we will grow.

This is a time of deep introspection, a gathering of authentic feeling and insight. We suffer the pain of transformation of ego domination. It's not a time for action—it's a time to go within, more deeply than ever before. There is a classic symbol in alchemy of a dragon biting its own tail, forming itself into a circle. This represents how we approach wholeness after the fermenting process has deflated the ego and the self has come together with its positive aspects into spiritual union.

In his book *The Emerald Tablet*, Dennis William Hauck defines Putrefaction as "the absolute suppression of ego ... often perceived as a dark depression in which the former ruling principle of the personality must die to make room for a higher identity."[8] This is a deeply creative process of being courageous enough to see all of our loathsome aspects without self-criticism, feeling sorry for ourselves as victims, reverting to infantile need-fulfilling behaviors, or misinterpreting what is really going on.

Often, we feel we've been thrown into transformation without having given permission. If we were to blithely say, "Gee, I think it's time to dive into my putrefaction today," it wouldn't be as effective or meaningful because our conscious mind would be in charge. It's the unconscious mind that holds what we need to know as we transform our lives. The experience sometimes feels like being tossed off a cliff into an abyss. It is in the abyss that we find our new reality. When we recognize that we are not being punished or rejected, we begin to see how Putrefaction-Fermentation is actually helping us release what no longer works. It also shows us our power in ways we may not have considered before. Try this meditation to see what you discover about how releasing old habits and attitudes opens doors to your inner gold.

Putrefaction-Fermentation Meditation

Close your eyes, perhaps while playing quiet music, and relax your body. Now bring forth an experience from your past that you've had difficulty releasing. Picture it, recall the details of it, and feel how difficult it has been to let go. Perhaps there is grief or guilt associated with it, making it feel impossible to release.

Consider what you would need to do to allow this issue to no longer be a part of your life—in other words, to let it die. The first part of the Putrefaction-Fermentation process demonstrates the issue's impact in your life so you see it clearly. It does this by presenting painful or repulsive aspects that you have been avoiding. The alchemist's fire is at work, and to us, as we go through this agonizing process, we feel that fire as emotional upset, anxiety, and fear of what will happen next.

---

8. Dennis William Hauck, *The Emerald Tablet* (New York: Penguin Books, 1999), 115.

As we meditate on all of this, we can begin to see how the distasteful aspects of our lives have served to protect and disguise what we are actually seeking as happiness, success, peace, and a loving heart.

An important and essential part of this meditation is to ask yourself honestly if you are willing to let go of the issue and all your beliefs surrounding it. If you hesitate, ask yourself why it's important to keep this in your life. Are you willing to let it die so positive and wonderful things can fill the space it's been holding? If you are, set a strong intention to release it, but this requires daily work, not only in meditation, but in your thoughts throughout the day.

In your meditations and journal, explore how this issue will die. Does it dissolve, burn up, fly away, or drown in a sea of spiritual waters? Or is it merely a process of watching it, day by day, become less and less important, and making space for the things that you truly want in your life? A clue that you are succeeding in this is when you have moments of unexpected joy, peace, or inspiration—you'll know then that the Putrefaction process is complete, and the old, unneeded, and distracting aspects that held you back have rotted away. As they did this, they formed a kind of consciousness compost in which Fermentation can now bring you to a totally new way of being. It brings inspiration into our lives and prepares us for the next stage of Distillation, where we become even closer to our authentic nature.

⟹◆⟸

As you work to allow negative aspects of yourself to die, think about whether you have ever sat with a person as they were dying. If so, it was unequivocally a major event in your life. To be witness to someone letting go of every aspect of human life is frightening to some, inspiring and deeply moving to others. Shocking, unnerving, beyond belief, filled with grace, this intense experience brings us face to face with the truth that we ultimately have no control over our mortality. Whether it is a person or an aspect of self that dies, it is a process of high evolution of Soul.

Equally mysterious and empowering is witnessing someone being born. You may have experienced the joy of having been fully awake as your child was being born, or the ineffable thrill of being present as your grandchild comes into the world. I witnessed my two daughters being born and was present at the births of my two granddaughters. I sat with my father and others as they died or were near death. Whether witnessing a Soul just entering an earthly life or leaving it, the experience is profound. Each experience with birth and death connects us to those births and "little deaths" we have throughout our lives.

When my teacher Brugh Joy died on December 23, 2009, I, like so many of his students, deeply grieved his passing. Many of us felt a part of ourselves had died. For me, Brugh's death was a Putrefaction-Fermentation experience since it awakened me to how, through the years of study with him, I tended to project onto him my disowned shadowy gifts and life purpose. His death confirmed to me that he was human, rather than the untouchable god I'd chosen to see him as for many years. The reality of his physical death helped me to perceive him as the incredibly bright, intuitive, astute, clever, humorous—and human—man that he was. As I emerged from the depths of grief, his teachings became what they were always meant to be rather than how I used to project my own aspects onto him. My projections died with him as I embodied his teachings of unconditional love, innate harmony, healing presence, and compassion.

Life is never created—it exists eternally. We merely create a way to experience it with all our senses. We create an illusory scenario that life begins with conception and birth, but the process merely shows us life in a way we can perceive it. A baby isn't a new life. Her appearance is merely a manifestation of ongoing life in form. The form alone is created, not life itself. Life is merely a revelation of the Divine in form.

This mystery of creation applies to death as well. In ancient Greek, when the first letter in the word *death* is removed, the word becomes "immortality." When it is time for a shift or change within the individual consciousness, the body's form dissolves, either slowly, with aging or disease processes, or quickly, as in an accident. It is only the form that dematerializes, never the life that animated or inspired the form. Life exists eternally and can never die. It's never "a matter of life and death." There is only life, even while our perception of it is cloaked by what seems to our human senses as annihilation of the whole being at death.

Bringing forth darkness into consciousness does not mean eliminating it or covering it with light, which is what most try to do. The transformational process is never about the exclusion of the dark. In trying to get rid of anything that frightens us, we miss the opportunity to explore, accept, and transform our perceptions. By courageously examining our fears, without running from them, we can discover deeper aspects within our unconscious minds. It is here that we can make profound changes, even though the process is formidable, because the more we learn about our inner depths, the more we become one with the consciousness from which we were created. By not avoiding or denying these powerful aspects of the deep self, we connect more consciously with our Soul.

Two years before I learned of my father's inoperable cancer, I had a powerful dream in which I am cleaning up his room. I begin opening curtains to let in the light. I am slightly irritated that the light has been kept out of the room. Suddenly a huge earthquake occurs. I run outside and see deep cracks in the ground all around me. The dream forecast that the inner work I'd been doing for so long had prepared me to assist him when he died. And later, in his actual dying process, I felt blessed to be his death midwife, offering ceremony, bringing in the light of spirit, and having the incredible experience of seeing his Soul, appearing as a cream-colored smoky swirl, leave his body through his crown. This affected my beliefs about the eternal nature of the Soul. I no longer doubted that the body is merely a vehicle for the Soul to use in a human lifetime.

It's now been over twenty-five years since my father died, yet on numerous occasions I have felt his presence and heard his voice, imparting deep wisdom that I could not have fully received while he was in a human body. While he was alive, I'd had no idea that he had so much to share. It was a delightful surprise when I read this passage from *Into the Light* by John Lerma, MD: "The more enlightened one is, the higher in the physical body that the soul is released. The highest is the top of your head."[9] Recalling how I'd seen his Soul swirl out of the crown of his head, I needed no further proof that my father still exists and that he is here for me as a teacher and friend.[10]

One self-test that can help you check your willingness to begin the process of dying to ways of the past is to pay attention to your body. When you experience something that differs from your known pattern, does your stomach clench? Does your heart start beating faster? Do you get an instant headache? Do you feel lightheaded? Do you feel that you must defend your old position? All of these are clues that your grip on an old belief is not what your Soul, your higher self, would have you believe. When the body signals like this, it is the Soul's voice, loud and clear, telling you that you need to let go, surrender, and die to whatever is holding you hostage to obsolete ways of being that do not reflect your inner gold. Though many of your beliefs and behaviors may have protected you early in life, they may no longer serve and need to be transformed. Like a road sign telling you there's a pothole—or worse—ahead, the body is warning you that if you aren't willing to change your perceptions, you will have great difficulty in changing your route to one you say you want to travel on.

The ancient Sumerian myth of the goddess sisters Inanna and Erishkigal demonstrates the essential nature of dying to our old concretized beliefs, attitudes, and behaviors—the ultimate alchemical *mortificadio* experience. It illustrates how we hold on to beliefs to protect ourselves from what we fear to change, and how we are ultimately moved toward final surrender to our Soul's purpose and our Philosopher's Stone.

Here is my interpretation of the myth.

---

9. John Lerma, MD, Into *the Light* (Franklin Lakes, NJ: Career Press, 2007), 72.
10. Nanci Shanderá, PhD, "Midwifing Death," *Shaman's Drum Magazine* (Fall 1988).

The goddess Inanna is an ineffective ruler in her land due to her greed and self-obsession. She's concerned with aging and appearance, she's fearful of losing her riches, and she neglects her kingdom. Her people are unhappy, food is scarce due to a long-term drought, and unrest is growing.

Her advisors tell her to seek help from her sister, Erishkigal, who is the queen of the underworld. Reluctantly, Inanna makes the trek through the desert to the caves that are her sister's kingdom. She stands at the entrance of the main cave and demands entry, but the guards will not allow her to proceed until she takes off her crown and leaves it with them. She is indignant and professes her regality, thinking that this will impress them to allow her inside. However, the guards stand firm and open the gate only when she finally relinquishes her crown, grumbling all the way.

At the second gate, she must give up her jewels; at the third, her cloak; and at the fourth, her robe. At the fifth, she must take off her dress, and at the sixth, her undergarments. Finally, she stands before the seventh gate totally naked. She moves, alone, into a large grotto that is lit by torches in wall sconces. When her eyes adjust to the light, she sees her sister, Erishkigal, sitting on her throne upon an altar made of skulls and bones.

Erishkigal glares at Inanna and growls, "Why have you entered my kingdom uninvited?"

Inanna tells her she needs her help because her kingdom is in ruins. Erishkigal responds by asking, "What are you willing to sacrifice?"

Inanna is taken aback, not expecting to have to give up anything to get what she believes is rightly hers. She says she will sacrifice nothing, and Erishkigal orders her guards to impale Inanna on an iron hook on the wall.

Time passes, Inanna's body rots, and the flesh falls to the ground, leaving only bones. Erishkigal orders her servants to take Inanna's body down and put her bones on a stone bier in the center of the grotto.

Erishkigal tells Inanna to review how poorly she has governed her people and to consider how this has affected the terrible situation they all find themselves in now. As merely a pile of bones, Inanna can do nothing, so she does as she is told. As she realizes what she has done, Erishkigal asks her again, "What must you sacrifice?"

As Inanna realizes she must sacrifice her self-obsession and greed, her body begins to grow back. It is still the same body, but she feels differently about it, seeing how her own wishes must now be relinquished and transformed for the good of her people.

Erishkigal tells her to go back to her kingdom and rule well, never forgetting the true meaning of sacrifice. Inanna moves back through the seven gates, collecting her clothing as she goes, including her jewels, which she will now use to make her people's lives better, and her crown, which she keeps as a symbol of right rulership. Inanna emerges from the cave as a good and effective queen, and her kingdom begins to thrive once again.

This story illustrates the difficulties in bringing the ego's protective defenses under our conscious control. We hold entrenched beliefs and won't consider the harm they do to others and to ourselves. Only when we are dragged, often kicking and screaming, into waking up can our lives truly change. The gates we must pass through are difficult and many times frightening, but they offer us opportunities to develop courage and strength of character. When at the bottom of our resources, the measure of our resistance or willingness forms the outcome. We either get "hung up" or we move on to a new way of being. It is through sacrificing our outdated protections, perceptions, beliefs, attitudes, and behaviors that we mature and become whole.

Putrefaction-Fermentation transforms old beliefs, whether personal or collective. Experiencing this stage reveals how narrow and limited your perceptions were, and how they were influenced by the ego as well as by the thoughts and beliefs of the collective unconscious that has existed throughout all time. When old beliefs no longer apply in your life, you realize your full potential and the value of your spiritual presence in the world. By embodying the four attributes of heart-level consciousness—unconditional love, compassion, restoration of harmony, and the healing presence—we are able to open our hearts completely to all of life, and to the presence of God within us.

Summary Points

- The alchemical stage of Putrefaction-Fermentation integrates lower levels of consciousness with the higher through high-intensity fire and ferment.

- Putrefaction is particularly difficult, because in it, we face our darkest aspects, but this heralds the release of the lower, ego-driven influences to make space for what wants to come forth as authenticity.

- Fermentation happens after Putrefaction has caused material or beliefs to decompose. Then a catalyst of some kind emerges, whether biological or emotional, and the Fermentation process begins. In an alchemist's lab, this mixture is transferred to another container, which is a personal metaphor for the newly developed self. The key is to allow this process to do its work, rather than avoiding or rejecting it.

- Putrefaction-Fermentation creates a rich compost of everything that has rotted and been transformed. From the compost emerges clear understanding and perception of our experience of the past and brings us into the present, where we begin to take on our wholeness.

- The processes of death and birth relate to this stage of alchemy because we must allow certain aspects of self to die before our gifted, authentic aspects can arise. This birth experience is not unlike the birth of a human being—it is not a new person coming onto the planet; it has always been what it is and just takes a new form.

- The dark aspects of the Putrefaction-Fermentation process are necessary, for within them, we learn what our fears are in order to transform them.

- Your body gives you messages by its reactions to what you are truly feeling or experiencing.

- The Sumerian myth of Inanna teaches us about the essential nature of dying to our old beliefs, attitudes, and behaviors by bringing the ego's defenses under our control. In alchemy, this would be referred to as the *mortificadio* experience.

- When we are presented with a powerful, transforming experience, we can choose to stay where we are or take the risk of doing whatever it takes to open to a new way of being.

CHAPTER 10

THE SHADOW KNOWS

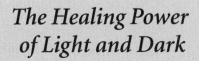

The Healing Power of Light and Dark

After experiencing the Putrefaction-Fermentation stage of alchemical transformation, we have learned that genuine transformation requires exploration of more than just the light aspects of consciousness. We deepen our work even further by exploring and integrating both light and dark forces. The darker aspect of personality—the shadow—is defined in Jungian psychology, as anything—an event, feeling, or person—that we deem bad or evil, or, conversely, unrealistically perfect. The shadow is whatever we reject and deny within ourselves, or project onto others. But no matter how strongly the shadow may hold these difficult aspects, it also holds our inherent gifts and talents that we're afraid to express.

Many spiritual seekers believe spiritual attainment means immersing themselves only in light and shunning or battling against the dark. This belief is based upon a value system of light as good and dark as bad. Inevitably, however, because nature always seeks balance, clinging to one polarity of belief plunges us into experiencing the opposite. This continues until we can restore the harmony between both poles. It's like riding a seesaw by yourself. You sit on one end while the other points skyward. To ride the other side of the seesaw, you run around, pull down the seat, and sit, only to remain on the ground again. Doing this repeatedly implies that there's something wrong with either the seesaw or with you. The answer is to sit in the center of the seesaw, which brings both sides into balance.

The shadow lives within all of us as individuals and as a collective. A sure indication that we are not paying attention to what the shadow can teach us is when we project our shadow onto others, just as a motion picture projector casts images onto a screen. Projection is when we see in others those things within us that we have most deeply rejected or denied. When we fear aspects within us, whether negative or positive, we release the tension by projecting the role of perpetrator or hero onto others. We are repulsed by those who do things we judge as bad or wrong, refusing to see our own reflection in their actions. And we fall in love with celebrities, believing that they are the kind of people with whom we'd be truly happy, while project-ing onto them the attributes that we believe we could never achieve.

Whether we revile or obsessively admire someone, the material we see in others, just as in dreams, is *about ourselves,* carefully hidden within us and denied as a part of us. What we project onto another may or may not actually *be* the reality of that person, but whether it is or not, it is never about *them.* It is *always* about us. And because our projections are illusory, our beliefs and perceptions about whomever we love or hate don't actually exist except in our minds and expec-tations. I've heard it said that whomever we're in love with doesn't exist—this, of course, referring to parts of ourselves that we reject and project upon others. The denouement comes when our partner shows his or her actual self and we feel betrayed and wonder what we ever saw in this person.

Throughout his classic book *Dark Night of the Soul,*[11] St. John of the Cross describes his descent into a dark abyss of unknowing after years of valuing only the light and rejecting the dark. What he discovers there is not the Devil, but his shadow, in all its varied textures and colors, at times appearing demon-like and dangerous, and at times angelic. St. John speaks to us about how our *perceptions* of suffering actually create it. Working with the shadow is a gift that can help us to withdraw the projections and transform our perceptions. In doing this, we see the projected aspects as parts of ourselves that need attention.

Centuries of religious and political programming have created the belief that anything dark is evil. This is the basis of racism and misog-yny, because people of color and women have been the targets of soci-ety's projected fears of the mysterious, shadowy regions of the collective unconscious. Examples of this collective projection are the Goddess religions and indigenous cultures and their spiritual practices and phi-losophies. Rejection of the dark feeds self-rejection and disrespect for

11. St. John of the Cross, *Dark Night of the Soul* (New York: Riverhead Trade Books, 2003).

Earth and her gifts. The way we have treated our Mother Earth reflects the ways we have treated one another and ourselves.

Denying our shadow causes us to run from it. Our society's increasingly frenetic tempo results as we run from what we are afraid to face, especially anything emotional or spiritual. We have distorted our inherent spirituality and feeling natures into the gods of materiality, greed, and misuse of power. Our modern attitudes about the arts reflect our rejection of the deep canyons of creativity within all of us for fear of its power. If we were to work with our shadow in concert with our Soul, we might have to sacrifice something. And that appears as too frightening for most of us. We may believe that our unique talents and preferences are not good for us. Maybe someone told us we'd never make a living as an artist or musician. So into the shadow those talents go. By agreeing with those who pass their fears along to us, we concretize the prejudicial beliefs that prevent us from being present with all our aspects. This compounds the repression of the shadow material and makes us a slave to our fears that we might have to face. Ignorance of the truth about the shadow leads us to infer that its contents could be nothing but monstrous. (Remember my *Poltergeist* dreams?) When we reject and unconsciously imprison uncomfortable emotions within the shadow, we lock away deep, secret desires that could bring joy and creative expression to our lives. Whatever lies in the dungeon of the unconscious is actually intended for our awakening and holds the gifts of balance and self-realization. The shadow is the womb of our consciousness…a dark, rich, and supple place that fertilizes the birth of all we hold within us.

When faced with the formidable descent into the shadow mysteries, the ego-protector may revolt or try to "make nice" to lure us away from changes that are beginning to occur. Author Diane Setterfield says, "Being nice is what's left when you've failed at everything else."[12] I've seen many people attempt to avoid the difficult parts of transformational work by throwing "white light" over what they fear. Basic

---

12. Diane Setterfield, *The Thirteenth Tale* (New York: Washington Square Press, 2006), 45.

physics proves that the brighter the light, the deeper the shadow. It's impossible to avoid what we fear. Even when we postpone the mindful process of facing the shadow material, crises arrive in our lives that guarantee pain and suffering until we settle down and do the work.

It takes maturity and determination to deal with the shadow forces. We must be willing to die to old beliefs by descending into an incubation period where we are bound, cocoon-like, within that which is dying. Remember what the caterpillar becomes in its cocoon? In our own process of metamorphosing we may feel like we've turned to jelly and have no direction, no power, and no idea of what is happening to us because our cherished beliefs are dissolving. This is an experience that cannot be intruded upon, and it is crucial not to be rescued. When little Johnny down the street pops a cocoon open to spy inside, the whole process ceases and the life inside it dies. When anyone who feels sorry for you, no matter how well intentioned, reaches out to help, your relief may actually stop your process. When darkness calls us, a mistimed application of light may interrupt, misinterpret, and even terminate the process. We must remain in our dismemberment in the cocoon jelly, allowing beliefs to be ripped apart without intervention, until we completely surrender to the changes that are occurring.

When we begin to peer out of our shadow cocoon, as if from a dark closet, we are blinded by a light that actually includes and embraces the darkness we've been traveling in. We feel temporarily disoriented by the new territory. We are filled with feelings and perceptions that seem strange and unfamiliar, but are, in actuality, our authentic feelings. They are unrecognizable because they have been disguised for so long and covered by protections that are no longer needed. Much of what has been protected is the opposite of our authentic feelings or gifts. The more submerged they are in the dark, the more difficult it is for us to redeem them and begin living our lives with those aspects intact. These are the parts of us that have been hidden in shadow but are, in most cases, our gifts and talents that we learned or were told early in life we shouldn't or couldn't involve ourselves in. Your shadow may be hiding and protecting your inner actor, musician, or teacher. When the shadow protects—unlike the ego's protection of things it has convinced you are wrong—it holds our gifts in trust for us until we are ready to dive into the shadowy regions of our mind to discover them. This exercise will help you see how self-judgments keep you from freeing the gifts the shadow has been safeguarding for you.

Discovering Your Shadow Exercise

Begin by making a list of behaviors and aspects that you secretly believe are "wrong" with you. Next to each write what you'd rather it be, an aspect of you that's always been difficult for you to express. Examples on this list might include: Spoiled Child—Mature Woman, "Good" Boy—Mature Man, Incompetent—Expert, Arrogant Know-It-All—Confident, Needy—Independent, Bad Mother—Wise Woman, Prideful—Self-Accepting, Conceit—Compassion, Guilt—Forgiveness, Pessimist—Optimist, and so on.

The first words on the list describe self-rejection. By considering these beliefs, you will begin to see how they served to protect you in the past. But when you are ready to let them go, through perhaps Calcination or Putrefaction-Fermentation, you make room for the hidden, preferable aspect to emerge from your shadow, which can make your life more authentic and connect you more closely to your Soul.

Examining each first word can teach you why the ego led you to believe this was true about you. For example, if you look at Bad Mother—Wise Woman, look at the judgment in the word *bad*. Look honestly within yourself: Do you really think you are bad in your mothering skills? Or have you picked up this idea from others' opinions? Have you compared yourself to the "perfect" mom presented in a woman's magazine article? Does "Bad Mother" reflect your authentic self, what you, deep down, sense to be the truth about you? You may discover this was a role you took on to protect yourself when you weren't sure of yourself as a new mother. You can review situations in which you believed you were being either a "Good" or "Bad" mother. The key here is to review this past experience without judgment, which cuts off learning potential. Next, imagine the same scenarios in ways that reflect who you are now. This requires not only non-judgment, but self-forgiveness as well. Let yourself appreciate how much you have grown.

Now, call up that opposite aspect from deep within your shadow self, which has held your hidden gifts for you until you were ready. "Bad Mother" can become the "Wise Woman" because self-judgment and forgiveness of old behaviors have been transmuted into wisdom and maturity.

Record all your insights in your journal. I recommend reviewing one of the positive words as descriptive of yourself just before you go to sleep.

———————

I've learned that both sides of my life issue of the conflict between arrogance and inadequacy actually sustained each other by overcompensating for the inherent weaknesses in both. I realized that my ego's job had been to protect my gifts of sensitivity and authentic power that my inadequate self was not yet capable of expressing and sustaining. When I was ready, I began working with the shadow, which surpasses the lower functions of the ego. Where the ego might have protected me from getting hurt with arrogance, the meaning of arrogance from the shadow standpoint was not about protection—it would have been more a veil for my acting, writing, or artistic talents until I was ready to bring them out of the shadow as gifts.

A good way to learn about your shadow is to observe who you criticize. As an example, do you dismiss actors, artists, or dancers? If so, what part of your creative expression are you denying? Do you disdain anyone who appears to have a successful career? If so, what is your definition of success and what is it about success that frightens you? Do you envy someone who has a fulfilling relationship? If so, what is it about deep intimacy that creates incomplete relationships in your life? These shadowy projections reveal your hidden dreams and desires, held in check by doubt, self-negation, and fear.

It's important to emphasize once again that *none* of the rejected aspects of ourselves is bad or wrong. What misleads us is our *perceptions* that the aspect is wrong. While rejecting my power by projecting it onto my spiritual teacher, I couldn't recognize my own gifts as a teacher. The value of shadow work leads us to see that if we can see it in others, we also have it in some form, unique to us, within ourselves. It may involve someone we admire who carries a characteristic similar to our own, or because of denial of our capacity for violence, it could lead us to ferocious judgment against a neighbor who kicks his dog.

Dr. Elisabeth Kübler-Ross was famous for saying that we all have both a Hitler and a Mother Teresa within us. We may not be outwardly abusive, but when we reject anything that doesn't align with our illusions of perfection or inadequacy, we are actually abusing ourselves with self-deception.

Many years ago, I began a relationship based upon my belief of the time that spiritual enlightenment meant jettisoning anything of a dark nature and emphasizing only the sweet and light. At a very romantic and fantasy-like party, I was profoundly drawn to a handsome, dark-haired man whom I found to be magnetic, mystical, brilliant, energetically powerful, and an avid reader of books on the mystical and the occult. Our whirlwind romance seemed like a fairy tale come true. I ignored clear signals that questioned his authenticity, such as his never having studied with a spiritual teacher nor gone through any type of inner work or therapy. Instead, I chose to see only the magical qualities of the relationship, and disregarded my projections of things I'd downplayed within myself onto him. In turn, he projected his fantasies onto me as a New Age princess of light. As the relationship progressed, I discovered that he had a mental disorder but refused medication. I began to see how we both projected onto one another the hope for a rescuer because of what we weren't allowing to come to consciousness within ourselves. After only a few months, I realized I could no longer ignore the projections of my shadow onto him, so I told him to leave. I knew he was only an illusion of what I had disowned by ignoring my own shadow elements. *Dis-illusion-ment* is the dismantling of fantasy projections.

The gift in this painful breakup lay in the valuable experience I gained in getting to know my shadow. About a year later, I chose the shadow as the theme of my graduate thesis. I also had what I call a completion dream, where we are shown how we work through a challenge and its resolution. In my dream, the man and I are in a wide, fast-moving river, which is flowing toward a huge waterfall, like Niagara. My boyfriend is floating behind me, and I keep turning to check on him and share my excitement. I become frustrated at my attempts to communicate with him since he keeps going under. Suddenly, the crosscurrent sweeps me off to the side and onto the bank as I watch him go over the falls. I am met by several loving people, who reach out and tell me to stand up. As I feel a wonderful connection to the earth, I feel relieved that the man is no longer with me.

When the shadow is brought to active awareness, it contributes greatly to our Distillation process because it helps us clarify who we are and what we are capable of. Now we distill those parts of us that have been refined in the previous stages of alchemical transformation. Just as we distill water to make it more pure, what we distill in our consciousness clarifies all that we have experienced so we can enjoy a deeper awareness of our innate wholeness.

Summary Points

- The Putrefaction-Fermentation stage of alchemy teaches us that transformation requires a balance of all aspects of consciousness, including and especially the light and the dark.
- The darker aspect of personality is referred to as the shadow, which is anything that we perceive as bad or imperfect, while in fact it's whatever we reject, deny, or project onto others and it can be either difficult material or our gifts and talents that we are afraid to express—it all becomes part of the shadow.
- Taking full, conscious ownership of our shadow material requires a sacrifice of some kind: beliefs, attitudes, actions toward ourselves

or others, or anything that we perceive as threatening to the way we are.

- Working with the shadow involves far more than making something "nice," putting white light around it, or running away from it. Because the shadow is actually a powerful ally for us, our task is to face it and learn to understand it.

- Working with the shadow requires full attention and an acceptance of the metamorphosis that we are going through. It is not a time to be rescued or pitied by others.

- When we have worked with the shadow, we are able to see the light in a different way than before—it's the light that has always included the darkness within it. Our shift into acceptance of the shadow, no matter whether it's presenting a new task of consciousness work or a new realization of our talents, leads us to a more realistic view of ourselves.

- Unlike the ego-protector, which builds walls against our growth, the shadow urges us, when we are ready, to explore and embody both dark and light within us, because it teaches us that both aspects are intended to empower us as our authentic selves.

- To learn about the shadow and how it functions, observe whom you criticize, either individuals or groups. Projection of the shadow is always about ourselves, not the other person.

- By taking ownership of our shadow, we assist the Distillation process, because knowing the shadow helps us clarify who we are and why we are here.

CHAPTER 11

Distillation

Refining the
True Self

*"Your feelings and thoughts are the feelings
and thoughts of the Whole Universe."*
~Alchemical Arcanum Five

The process of alchemical *Distillation* involves a rising up from the depths of the lower work and developing a balanced relationship with both the higher and lower aspects of being. The process requires a sacrifice of beliefs that have held us in self-absorption, concerns about past and future, and false perceptions of life. An authentic sacrifice—meaning to do or make something sacred—moves us into a refined, pure essence of selflessness and a fuller awareness of life. This is not an easy process, because we must go through Distillation many times before we achieve the distinct qualities of a truly distilled consciousness. When alchemists work in this stage, they must continually repeat the laboratory processes over and over before they gain the essence they have been working for. They believe that repeating this process will eventually release the spiritual substance within the materials they've been working with. And when they have finally created this substance, they know they are nearing Coagulation, the last stage of alchemical transformation.

From a personal alchemical standpoint, repeating the process brings us closer than ever to our spiritual self, but because it's so new or even foreign, we may feel lost and disoriented because our perception of life has changed dramatically. Distillation is a deeply spiritual experience, and no matter how much we've meditated or studied through the years, this process takes us much deeper into a clear and unified consciousness with the Divine. When we become spiritually and emotionally distilled, we merge with the collective conscious and unconscious without the distractions of the past. Ego no longer controls us, its energy having become a partner in strength. We can appreciate the mysteries of the collective, as well as personal shadow material, without the ego's interference or emotional reactivity. We have become deeply conjoined in body and Soul—Earth and Heaven; as above, so below. Our wholeness is nearing completion, so in everything we do, say, think, and feel, we are unable to regress to the old ways of being.

The process of Distillation is built upon the complete surrender of our fears of past and future that block access to our full consciousness. Individuals and nations are motivated by events of the past and imagined events of the future. Certainly, it's important to explore personal and global history, but if our intention is to prove how awful life is rather than to transform our perceptions so we can expand our ability to love, we will continue to re-create what our fears would have us believe. It takes courage to distill our negativities in order to break new ground.

If we perceive consciousness as spherical, rather than linear, we create a new way of relating to past and future because everything in a sphere occurs simultaneously—there is no beginning or end within a sphere. Hierarchical thinking is replaced by cooperation within such a paradigm. This may mean that past and future events are occurring at the same time and actually become the present moment. The theory of retro-causality poses the possibility that events in the future affect those from the past. It may be possible that when we work to transform ourselves through prayer or meditative work, we affect not only our future but our past as well. And the more we shift from a belief in past and future into one of a unified field of consciousness, where everything happens at once, perhaps the events of the past or future may not take place at all or in the same way if we work with them as if they were all occurring in the present. Could it be that as we transform our lives, we become so much more authentic than we were in the past that we realize the past is built upon belief and not actuality? This is what may happen in the process of Distillation.

Just as water is distilled to remove impurities, the stage of Distillation purifies our consciousness and frees us from linear perceptions of past and future. In the beverage industry, various fermented solutions are distilled to produce a higher alcohol content, making them stronger. We can relate this to transformational work in how, after various areas of our lives have been putrefied and fermented, they become more refined and potent through Distillation. Because our energies have been cleansed and cleared, Distillation prepares us for the entry of the higher personal and universal forces that will ultimately conjoin with the lower ones to bring about wholeness. When you become distilled, you are grounded in both the earthly and spiritual worlds simultaneously. You have matured, no longer expecting life to meet egoistic expectations, and have released belief in negative self-regard. You live in the present moment, not worrying about past mistakes or future possibilities. The shift in consciousness results in not focusing on those things any longer because you now believe that you create your reality based upon your thinking—either negative or positive. And by the time you've reached your Distillation, you're no longer interested in nor able to create negative experiences because you now know the value of staying grounded in the positive.

Distillation requires the sacrifice of fear in favor of becoming spiritually unified and benefiting the greater good. To live in fear of the past and future is to live a life of illusion. The past is no longer present except in our memory, and the future is what we make from millisecond to millisecond as we move through our day. And as the future appears in our present moment, it instantly becomes the past. Clearly, the task is to live in the present moment. This is difficult for most everyone, since we are conditioned to anticipate the future or regret our past.

Here are several Distillation meditations to help you disconnect from fear-based patterns, to deepen awareness of your connection with the Divine, and to integrate it with your earthly experience. The more you repeat these exercises, the more you will distill old beliefs and fears. These meditations stimulate imagery, a very effective transformative tool. By imagining clearly, you are using a very powerful spiritual law. The clearer your image, the quicker it will manifest. Open yourself as much as you can to what comes forth from your meditations. They can have healing, empowering, and long-lasting effects.

DISTILLATION MEDITATION #1: THE SILVER TOWER

Close your eyes, listen to quiet music, and imagine moving into the entrance of a tall, silver tower whose walls contain symbols of birds, stags, and flowers as well as symbols of death and resurrection. Depending upon your religious background, you may see typical Judeo-Christian scenes, or something quite unique to your own cosmology—or perhaps something you've never imagined before.

Begin to ascend a circular staircase, and continue to observe everything around you. When you reach the top of the tower, you will see a rainbow, whose light illumines the tower. This is water that is distilled by light. Allow yourself to feel the presence of a Divine being, and then listen to what it wants to tell you about your distilled (purified, clarified) purpose in this lifetime. As you listen, become aware that you recognize this being as your higher self, your Soul, that is speaking to you.

Allow this being to merge with your energy field and physical body. You may feel it as it comes into you. You may have physical sensations as this happens. Be aware of how you feel and what thoughts come into your mind.

Sit for a few minutes feeling this integration, experiencing it and embodying it. When you feel complete, go back down the tower the same way you ascended, then write the experience in your journal.

Distillation Meditation #2: Integrating Past and Future with the Present

Sit comfortably, eyes closed, breathing easily. Allow any pleasurable past experiences that arise to float across your awareness. Next, call forth your hopes and dreams about the future. Allow these past and future ideas to float freely. Feel the happy times and embody the feelings of joy. Feel them filling your body and mind with health. Embrace the feelings of a future filled with freedom and creativity. Now begin to bring these feelings from past and future into the present moment so that they become alive, close and near to you. Let them be a part of what nourishes and strengthens you *now*, not only at some distant time in the future or the past.

DISTILLATION MEDITATION #3:
CHANGING YOUR PERCEPTIONS OF YESTERDAY

This is a meditation in which you move into the timeless, space-less arena of non-locality. After seating yourself comfortably and closing your eyes, breathe deeply for several minutes, and allow yourself to think spherically rather than in the usual linear way. You'll use *inclusive thinking* rather than space-time–related thinking.

When you are deeply relaxed and focused, allow events in which you made mistakes or missed opportunities to float into your mind's eye. Be aware of how you've always thought of them: life-shattering, proof of your unworthiness, depressing, etc. Now imagine a veil between you and those experiences of the past. On one side are the mistakes, and on the other is your Observer self, sitting in your chair in the present moment.

Now set a strong intention to allow the gifts in all those experiences to come forth. When you know you are willing to allow this, imagine the veil dropping. See them all as if with different eyes, reviewing one at a time, discovering the gifts they gave you, and spending enough time with each to fully realize how it was your perception that caused you to be emotionally crushed by these experiences. Give thanks to the lessons that made you strong, the suffering that gave you compassion, and the challenges to your self-esteem that constructed self-appreciation.

What you are doing is distilling your cherished convictions about your past, your limited evaluations of yourself, and the calcified beliefs that have held you hostage until now, so you can see them from a different and more mature perspective. (An important note here: Attempting to change your past just to feel better will not be effective, because the point is to free yourself from negative beliefs, especially if they feel uncomfortable as you are transforming them. Discomfort signals something is changing, but continued discomfort means that you are resisting the change that wants to happen or something that wants to be revealed.)

Before completing this meditation, once again thank and embrace each event or person and express gratitude for the gifts they have given you. The more you repeat this exercise, the more you will distill your past so you can embody the original purpose of the experiences. Feel the freedom from your *perceptions* of the past and your new perceptions based in the present moment. Pay particular attention to any insights or senses you receive, for they may be leading you to more clarity about your Soul's purpose and will become even clearer the next time you repeat the meditation.

DISTILLATION MEDITATION #4:
THERE IS NO FUTURE—THERE IS ONLY NOW

Sit comfortably, close your eyes, begin slow, easy breathing, and imagine a scene from nature that you love. It could be your garden, an arboretum you like to visit, or a campsite you return to each year. Look around you and begin to focus on a favorite tree or plant. See, hear, and feel its presence and aliveness. Do this with a deep sense of being in the present moment with this plant. Slowly, begin to consider what has brought this plant to where it is at this moment: What happened in its past to allow it to grow and bloom? Did someone buy it at a nursery and plant it? Did the wind blow a seed that planted itself in the ground? How did it survive? Watering, rain, fertilizer? Be aware that this plant had a past, but is no longer in it, and because it is only in this present moment, it has no future. This is so because each present moment keeps happening so there is never a future, only present moments. The plant's past made it what it is today and the future is right now in the beauty of the plant.

As you realize these truths about the plant, try the same meditation over again, only this time using yourself as the subject. When you are complete, what do you now know about your past and future and the power of the present moment?

Distillation Meditation #5: Remodeling the Past, Embracing the Present Moment

Prepare yourself for deep meditation in whatever way works best for you. Relax, close your eyes, breath rhythmically, and clear out distracting thoughts.

Now imagine two houses next to each other. One is the house you're moving out of and the other is the one you're moving into.

Begin in the old house. Look around at all you have accumulated in your environment there. You may see things you actually have that have certain meaning, or things symbolic of aspects of yourself you have outgrown. Pack boxes with things you'll take with you, and other boxes of things you'll donate to charity, an appropriate action for being willing to let go of your past. As you pack, feel how willing you are to release the house and the many things in it that, if kept, would continue to hold you back from your new and expanding purpose.

Watch the charity truck drive up and the workers loading it with your donations. As you watch these items or symbols leaving your life, affirm that since they served you in your past, they will serve others as well—as a kind of compost for their growth, too.

Now a moving van appears, and the things you plan to take with you to your new house are loaded into this truck. Check to make sure you really want to take each of the items or symbols. Be non-critically aware of the number of items in both trucks. If you change your mind about anything on the moving van, just ask the movers to put it in the charity truck.

After everything has been moved out of your old house, do a walk-through, feeling the emptiness in it and giving thanks to it for having housed you for so long. You might want to leave a flower or some expression of gratitude for the house's support of you in your past.

Now turn your attention toward the new house. Take in all its beauty and freshness. Admire its structure, its angles, and the way the light touches it and creates both shadows and sparkling reflections. Look at all its windows and doors, its well-constructed walls, its lush gardens, pools and fountains, trees blowing gently in the breeze, and strong, sturdy roof.

Feel and see yourself walking confidently up the front walkway, smelling the flowers along its borders and sensing excitement about moving in.

As you unlock the front door and enter, you turn and look once more at the old house, which now feels distant and detached from who you are now in your new home. Walk into the living room and feel the thrill of seeing your new fireplace—the hearth, which is the heart of your home—and the lovely colors on the walls. Wander through the rest of the rooms and bless them as you go.

Now the movers are bringing in whatever belongings you chose to keep. You show them which rooms to place everything in and you silently give thanks that you have brought such a rich and varied number of experiences from your past that have made you what you are.

Thank the movers as they leave. Begin putting all of your things away—or if you brought nothing, sit and meditate on what you wish to bring into this new home. This home is a symbol of who you have been becoming all your life. This is a place of great peace and joy and is the place of your Soul. You have come home to reside with your inner gold.

⇒◦⇐

The Distillation arcanum says, "Your feelings and thoughts are the feelings and thoughts of the Whole Universe." We all have an undeniable connection with every part and manifestation of creation. Wholeness and enlightenment come about as a direct result of having embodied this spiritual truth. The energy field that surrounds every individual thing in the universe is the same field that embraces you. As you settle into your distilled life, you will become more aware and appreciative of literally being a part of the unified field of consciousness that lives and thrives in everything and everyone.

Summary Points

- Distillation is the process where we have developed a balanced and whole relationship with the higher and lower aspects of our being. To succeed in this stage, we must sacrifice beliefs and attitudes of self-centeredness, fear of past and future, and perceptions of ourselves and others that are illusory rather than authentic.

- Distillation must be experienced over and over until we are completely refined in the purest state of consciousness—the one we were originally created to have.

- Though Distillation brings us closer to our spiritual reality, we may feel disoriented because our lives have now changed so dramatically. We have merged with the collective consciousness, our ego no longer controls us, we are partners with our shadow, and we have become conjoined in the physical and the spiritual: Earth and Heaven; as above, so below.

- Successful Distillation means we have surrendered our fears of the past and future that have always blocked us from our true spirit.

- A distilled person perceives consciousness as spherical rather than linear, where there is no beginning or end. Cooperation of all of our aspects has become a natural way of being. Past and future blur into a consciousness of present, and the distilled person lives in the now moment.

- After many experiences in Distillation, we're no longer involved in creating or believing in negative experience because we now know the value of living in the positive.

CHAPTER 12

LIVING THE DISTILLED LIFE

The Soul as Our Guide

After we have gone through our Putrefaction-Fermentation experiences, whatever has been boiled down to its essence by now is further purified in a process of using fire and condensation in Distillation, whose result is a more highly purified consciousness. In an alchemist's lab, after the liquid substance has been fermented, it is repeatedly washed and eventually is condensed into what the alchemists call the "Mother of the Stone." In our personal alchemical process, our consciousness has been concentrated to such a degree that we experience it as a non-ordinary event or state of consciousness. It may feel like a mystical or paranormal experience and one in which we may feel reborn—we have merged with the "Mother of the Stone" in a symbolic birthing experience in preparation for the next stage of Coagulation, where we may create our Philosopher's Stone. This is the balancing process of Distillation, which, like the alchemist's laboratory experiment of alternating burning and condensing a substance, moves us back and forth between any parts of our consciousness that have not been totally purified. For example, we may feel that Distillation has brought us to a high spiritual state, only to experience the resurgence of the ego's need for control. This may disappoint us or make us believe we didn't really reach the realm within Distillation. What is actually happening is that the aspects of us that never were fully born into our reality are now moving through the birth process, which ebbs and flows, contracting us while expanding us into new states of mind. Once Distillation has completely purified us after many experiences of it, we become balanced, open to all our inner gifts, and undeniably and consciously unified with the Divine. Our relationship with our Soul self is expanded, and we have far more access to inner guidance and insight than ever before.

Long before I went through all the Distillation experiences later in my life, I didn't always listen to my inner guidance. Its voice was overshadowed by my Inner Critic, an aspect of the ego-controller, which determined my outlook and actions while stifling or repressing parts of me. I would eventually learn that the purpose in this was to keep me from being hurt by rejection, the issue I'd come into this lifetime to resolve. If the Critic could guard me from expressing creatively, doing work I loved—even loving others—I wouldn't be vulnerable to criticism.

Some time ago while meditating, an image emerged in my mind's eye of a large, transparent, dark sphere, hovering in front of me. I felt drawn to it, so I imagined myself floating into it and sitting quietly. Through its dark walls I could see a sky filled with stars. The energy in the sphere impressed upon me how my attitudes and beliefs about myself were what was creating my suffering. I realized that my destructive feelings about myself and not listening to inner guidance had caused my self-criticism. I saw how my chronic depressive tendency held me back from getting hurt. I began to consider that my perceptions about my depression as a negative aspect sealed off what the depression might be able to teach me. So I put the depression in the sphere and listened to what it had to say. Because depression had lasted so long in my life, it took several sessions in the sphere before I understood its message. But when I did, it opened a whole new way of perceiving depression. It became a barometer of my beliefs about my life. I learned that the deep, shadowy part of me had been trying to get my attention, but it had turned to depression because I had been listening to the Critic rather than the shadow itself. Because my true desires and talents were not being given permission to express, what the shadow had been holding in trust for me manifested as depression due to the influence of the ego-protector. The shadow told me in the Sphere Meditation how the gifts within me were needing attention and expression. The transformation of depression to self-expression didn't happen overnight—it took time but was invaluable in healing the depressive cycle.

Since I have been using this meditation for years now because it works so well to guide me in what my ordinary mind was not allowing me to see, I am able to access what Distillation had formulated for me in terms of clarity of understanding and confidence in whatever action was required. Here is how you can use this meditation as a way to stay connected with your experience in Distillation.

THE SPHERE MEDITATION

First, define what is troubling you. You may not know precisely what it is, but just use whatever arises: a feeling, a thought, an experience. Now, sit quietly, eyes closed, and breathe rhythmically.

Next, imagine the issue as a large, *transparent* sphere, the color of whatever you are experiencing; in most cases, it will be a dark color. (I emphasize imagining the dark sphere as clear and transparent to represent a new way of experiencing the dark as clear rather than what we've been taught to believe.) I strongly suggest that you allow it to be dark because it clearly represents how you are feeling. Attempting to put pink on pain doesn't work!

Now imagine yourself sitting in a meditative posture and floating into the sphere. As you reach the center, stop and just hover there. Allow yourself to completely *feel* the feelings about your issue, but without expressing them outwardly. You will learn more about your feelings if you go *into* them without conveying them. Keep your focus on the feelings themselves without allowing them to pull you off purpose. Certainly feel your feelings so you can identify them, but don't react to them in your usual way. Be an observer rather than becoming entangled within them.

As you float within the sphere, feeling the feelings, ask the sphere to teach you of the purpose of the issue. Ask this question *unconditionally*, without expectations of what it might tell you. Let go of being in charge. Let the sphere teach you without interruptions. If your ego-protector tries to intrude, firmly tell it to wait outside, that you will deal with it later. Listen for as long as you can; then, even if you don't get a clear answer this time, give thanks to the sphere-issue, and imagine yourself floating back out and into your body.

Open your eyes and record your experience in your journal. If you haven't received anything consciously, set your intention to try again at another time. Keep in mind that you have stirred your inner pot, so the answer may come in a dream, an insight, or an experience outside the sphere.

The key to this meditation is to listen deeply, humbly, and without defenses. It is in deep listening that you will feel, sense, see, or hear the answer and begin to understand the purpose of the issue. Through practicing this meditation, you will learn to recognize how holding on to conditions prevents awareness and transformation of issues.

⟫⟫◆⟪⟪

Becoming completely distilled requires deep and repetitive review of our beliefs, such as low self-worth. Any negative belief draws energy out of positive ones and prevents authentic distillation from occurring. Our bodies may express this energy leak through exhaustion, our emotions may overwhelm us, and our problems may seem insurmountable. While we're trying to pull ourselves back together and feel secure, the energy we need to accomplish this may not be available. We may reach out to others for security and unknowingly attempt to use *their* energy to fill in our gaps. This deepens the feeling of insecurity because others can usually sense when their energy is being siphoned off so they avoid contact. What we can't see when we're feeling panicky and alone is that it's not the absence or presence of others that creates our security—it's something we're not aware of that resides within ourselves.

It takes time and dedication to create authentic change. It requires taking risks, but taking them may move us closer to a loving relationship to self and Soul. Isaac Newton took a risk by staring into the sun so he could explore light. Medieval alchemists ingested mercury to discover its qualities. Modern quantum physicists imperil their reputations by presenting new, heretical ideas about how the universe works. And you and I dig into things about ourselves that others warn us against because it makes others uncomfortable about themselves when we make changes.

Maybe you've stepped over your own boundaries—or allowed others to step over them—and been yelled at for doing things the wrong way, felt panicked and lost and alone, or believed you could never be good enough or successful enough. But these painful experiences lead us to discover opportunities for healing within adversity. We become the alchemists of our Souls. The gold has always been there, and we are enriched if we risk going through the fire to find it. And when we reach the full experience of Distillation, we are spiritually and emotionally mature enough to merge with the collective conscious and unconscious without becoming devastated by what we find there. Now the ego no longer controls us and we can therefore appreciate the mysteries of the collective and personal shadow material without the ego's intrusion. One of my Distillation experiences presented a truth I'd never known before. I had been taking time off from work due to deep exhaustion and had no energy to do much more than sleep, watch a little TV, or read. The rest of the time, I stared at the ceiling, meditating. For some time I had been praying for joy, peace, and serenity. These attributes always seemed so distant and impossible for me to have in my life. But suddenly, during meditation, I felt joy, peace, and serenity, and realized that I'd *always* had them within me all along. I just didn't know it because the ego-protector kept me from feeling and experiencing them.

Distillation frees our creativity and connects us deeply with the Divine aspects of ourselves. It heralds the entry of the influence of the higher forces and the balancing of those forces with the lower ones. This provides groundedness, an essential key to wholeness. A distilled person doesn't expect life to meet egoistic expectations, nor does she view it as a devastating disappointment when it doesn't meet those expectations. Most importantly, a distilled person would know that her golden Soul, rather than the ego, is now guiding her life. This stage of alchemical transformation prepares us for the most important stage of *Coagulation*, where we *live* from our Soul selves with no intrusion by the ego any longer. It is the stage when we have no doubt who we are and why we are here. We know our purpose, and we know how we are being asked to serve others and the planet. In the next chapter, we explore Coagulation, what it is, how it is reached in consciousness, and how it exemplifies the Divine within us. In the final chapter, I offer one of my own experiences of Coagulation, as an example of how a lifelong challenge can be transformed through the use of the alchemical levels, and then finally the condensing, unifying, and coagulating embodiment of singular consciousness with the universal.

SUMMARY POINTS

- Using a combination of repeated fire and condensation, the Distillation stage results in a highly purified consciousness. Our consciousness is concentrated so we may begin to have non-ordinary or mystical events and states of consciousness. The necessity of repetition in this stage is to guarantee full and complete purification of consciousness. We may slip back and forth between the ego's influence and the distilled state, and this occurs to the degree that we were not fully born into our earthly reality. When complete, our distilled self is equally present with both earthly and heavenly realities.

- By using the Sphere Meditation, we can learn directly what our challenges are trying to teach us..

- The Distillation process challenges us to not be drawn into negative thought or action. We may tend to reach out to others for security during this disorienting time, but being rescued during this process is the last thing we need—it pulls us away from what we are being taught.

- Though we must face and overcome various obstacles on the path, by the time we are fully engaged with the Distillation process we have matured emotionally and spiritually, so we are not undone or devastated when we meet new experiences that shock and surprise us.

- A distilled person has surrendered expectations and thus is not disappointed when life isn't what he or she might have wanted it to be before Distillation. The distilled person knows the ego no longer controls his or her life and refers to the Soul for guidance, understanding, and inspiration.

CHAPTER 13

Coagulation

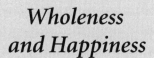

Wholeness and Happiness

"The Stone is a purified consciousness that remains intact on all levels of reality."
~Alchemical Arcanum Seven

In alchemy, a coagulated person is a complete, whole being whose consciousness on all levels, whether physical, mental, or emotional, is spiritually integrated. This person has discovered what alchemists call the Philosopher's Stone, the quintessential proof of alchemical enlightenment, by having traveled through all the stages, over and over, until the whole being is perfected. As arcanum seven says, one with a purified, or coagulated, consciousness lives in a reality where reactivity and fear have been replaced by a genuine, solid belief in unity with higher consciousness, the Divine.

I'll repeat here what I said in the introduction: We don't gain the Philosopher's Stone—higher consciousness—easily. We have to fight through and earn it by working all the alchemical processes of transformation: incinerating the ego's control; redeeming emotion and intuition; discovering discernment and wisdom; opening the heart through balancing the inner masculine and feminine; integrating lower levels of consciousness with the higher through fire and ferment; distilling all the work already done and developed to a pure essence; and surrendering into a new consciousness of wholeness. Every one of these processes requires a sacrifice, generally consisting of old, outdated, and cherished beliefs.

By learning to exchange old, fear-based attitudes and perceptions for new, life-giving ones, we enter the *Mystery of Sacrifice*. This is a profound and essential element of spiritual transformation, but most think of it as something melodramatic (you know, the diva sweeping the back of her hand theatrically across her brow!), an atonement, or a requirement for penance. The actual definition of the word *sacrifice* is "to make sacred." True sacrifice transmutes less developed levels of consciousness into an awakened state. In most cases, sacrifice requires that the ego's desires, protections, and controls are relinquished for the greater good.

In an episode of the television series *Eli Stone*, Sigourney Weaver's character of a deity tells Eli, who is resisting using his psychic gift: "A gift is something that is given. You don't own it ... the world does. And the world is asking you to use it ... and you don't get to say no, no matter how much you might want to."[13] Eli must sacrifice his own personal desires for the good of humanity.

As we grow, we bump into "mirror people" along the way. They may be a therapist, parent, spiritual teacher, grandparent, or authentic friend, who reflect back to us what we most need to see about ourselves. We may feel disillusioned and betrayed if they don't act according to our expectations, such as when they don't rescue us. But expectations are often based upon unresolved infancy-childhood needs, and become inaccurately focused upon outer authority figures. This is not to say that a therapist or teacher doesn't actually hold the aspects we project onto them. It does mean, however, that the projection will hold us in stasis until we can withdraw the projection. When we reach a point in development that no longer requires the rejection of inner material by placing it outward, our perceptions of the mirror people change as they are sacrificed for the good of our Souls and of others.

Sacrifice is an offering to Spirit and can atone (remember the meaning of *atonement:* "being at one with") for actions and events of the past, and restructure energies positively. By repurposing our past, we contribute to the healing and transformation of collective, negative portals—energetic rips in the fabric of life. These energetic doorways are opened by those who act in ignorance, misuse their power, and renounce or ignore spiritual laws. On a collective level, global catastrophes, interpreted by a negative collective agreement and stimulated by the media, affect us far more than we are aware. I call this the "Hiroshima Effect." The unprecedented bombings of Japan in World War II by the United States cracked open the entire world to thoughts, beliefs, and behaviors previously unheard of and unacceptable, and escalated the collective misunderstanding and demonizing of the shadow. We

13. Eli Stone, ABC television episode, December 16, 2008.

deny and reject it, calling it bad, sinful, evil, etc., while we project it onto other societies that we refuse to understand or accept as part of the global community.

Though we have good intentions, we can still contribute to negative energies within the collective by ignoring or downplaying the importance of inner work. When we are traumatized by events in our lives and do nothing to restore balance, believing we are victims, we energetically confirm the conviction of victimization within the global mind. When an old house is being remodeled, old memories and energies of times and people gone by are stirred up as the walls are ripped off and the foundation is repurposed. Without conscious awareness of how our traumas affect everything in profound, far-reaching ways, combined with the belief that we have been harmed by others and the refusal to sacrifice those beliefs, we are haunted by the effects of negativity that radiate through our lives. Elizabeth Gilbert, author of *Eat, Pray, Love,* writes: "... I can see exactly where my episodes of unhappiness have brought suffering or distress or (at the very least) inconvenience to those around me. The search for contentment is, therefore, not merely a self-preserving and self-benefitting act, but also a generous gift to the world. Clearing out all your misery *gets you out of the way.* You cease being an obstacle, not only to yourself but to anyone else. Only then are you free to serve and enjoy other people."[14]

In indigenous societies, the medicine person or shaman of the tribe or clan restores balance by performing a healing ceremony or Soul retrieval for the afflicted but involving the whole group in the process. Practices like these are based upon the belief that *everything* we do, think, say, and feel affects all life on our planet and in the universe.

I want to repeat: *Everything* we do, say, think or feel has an effect on ourselves and others. When something is to be renewed, revised, remodeled, rebuilt, reformed, rectified, repaired, restored, or rejuvenated, it requires a sacrifice, whether simple or profoundly difficult. Specifically, it requires engagement with the heart, or else it is not an

---

14. Elizabeth Gilbert, *Eat, Pray, Love* (New York: Penguin Books, 2006), 260.

authentic and complete sacrifice. True sacrifice requires love—of self and others.

Some of us are empathic, which can be difficult because we may feel others' pain twice as greatly as our own. The key is learning the difference between our own feelings and reactions and those of others so we transmute their suffering rather than taking it on as our own. This has always been a challenge for healers and caregivers because of their empathic nature. But it is a higher work when we can focus on the other's highest truth. This frees them to face their own issues without having been rescued by our taking on their pain.

Once, I told the man I'd been in relationship with my reason for breaking it off with him. I told him that I had, unknowingly and empathically, been acting out his emotions in addition to my own. This is common with empathic people who must learn techniques to protect themselves from energy that does not belong to them. At the same time, they must be able to remain open and compassionate toward others. A wise rule when working with others' pain and suffering is to do what you can compassionately, but don't take on what they aren't willing to do for themselves. In his book *Owning Your Own Shadow,* author Robert A. Johnson writes: "To refuse another's shadow, you don't fight back, but like a good matador you just let the bull go by ... To be in the presence of another's shadow and not reply is nothing short of genius."[15]

When anyone finds herself in the *nigredo*—the alchemical term for deep, dark, difficult inner work, a dark night of the Soul—it may require solo work and not calling in someone to assist. Or if help is truly required, it is best to work with someone who knows her or his way around the underworld within us—that place that holds the shadow and untapped power. It is a place of periodic inner exploration, not a place to take up residence, because we need balance between the dark and the light to realize and sustain wholeness. The task in exploring the dark realms is not to make them "nice," for this

15. Robert A. Johnson, *Owning Your Own Shadow* (New York: HarperCollins, 1993), 36–37.

impedes transformation, but to establish a healthy balance between dark and light.

It is our state of consciousness that determines our experience. When we believe in fear as a fact, a frightening experience becomes our reality. We make agreements with fear by closing our hearts, judging others or ourselves, comparing ourselves with others, having unreasonable expectations of others and ourselves, maintaining predetermined and unquestioned beliefs, needing to be right, refusing change, being close-minded, refusing to sit patiently with ambiguity, thinking ahead about what we want to say rather than truly listening to others, being reactive, and taking offense.

Fear prevents change by sabotaging our intention to grow. A woman in one of my women's intensives was uncomfortable with the other women's sharing regarding sacrifice. She sat silent and was obviously upset. She told me later that she believed the others weren't centered in their hearts. She was unconscious to her own closed heart because of her fear that if she opened it, she would break down and cry and the other women would judge her—and that had always been unacceptable behavior to her. As we talked, she realized this was a lifelong pattern of unhealthy sacrifice of her valuable feelings for the fear of what others would think of her.

On the last night of the intensive, she dreamed that her job has been downsized and someone else has been hired in her place. She considers speaking to her boss, but decides to quit because she feels disrespected and unappreciated. While waiting for an elevator, her boss appears and tells her he doesn't want her to leave her job. The boss represents her ego-protector, in the guise of an understanding and supportive person, who complements her on her stoicism, but in reality the ego-protector, as the boss, serves to drag her back into the "old job" of repressing her feelings.

The dream helped her shift her fear so that she could make her act of sharing her tears and fears with the group a sacred act—a sacrifice of the protection of the ego and the belief that her job had defined her. The dream announced that a part of her was already moving away from the old patterns of rejecting her feelings. She shared her dream with the group, and the women supported her openly and shared that they had the same hidden fears about their own feelings. This was a surprising revelation to her.

In another group intensive a few months later, she shared a dream that illustrated how her heart had been opening since the last gathering. In the dream, she is wandering, feeling lost and invisible. She feels as though no one sees her, so she tries to make eye contact with others but to no avail. She enters an old, dilapidated, abandoned building, and sees a woman thirty feet underwater with a knife in her heart. She tells others and they retrieve the dead woman, who is wrapped in a cocoon-like membrane, which they split open.

She feared the dream was announcing something ominous, such as death or disease. This is a common reaction to dark dreams when we automatically jump to fear-based conclusions. This engrained habit gets in the way of our being able to dive deep into the rich symbology of our dream life and other powerful experiences.

In the dream, this woman's feeling of invisibility gives us a clue as to what is about to happen: old beliefs about her feelings are dissolving in preparation for a rebirth. Since structures in dreams generally represent how we perceive ourselves, the abandoned building represents the lifelong rejection of a strong emotional sensitivity. The entry is the birth canal that leads to the womb-like cocoon containing the stabbed woman. She is the dreamer's fear-induced deadening of feelings. The knife in the heart represents its requisite opening. The images in this dream must be shocking in order to generate enough energy to jettison old beliefs and inject new life force.

We can transform our own old beliefs by being willing to face difficult emotions or situations from the past or present. The woman who had the dream was able to face her previously unacceptable feelings by realizing her heart was opening. In the next exercise, you will learn how to do this, too.

SACRIFICE AND SOUL EXERCISE

Look at something you really want to do but are afraid to try. Ask yourself what you would have to release in order to do what you want to do. Then observe your emotional reaction to that. If it fills you with more fear, based on what you think might happen if you try, dive deeper into that feeling, watching carefully for anything that makes it seem like you would be diminished or put at risk by the act of releasing or giving it up.

Now ask the same question but this time seek an answer from your heart, such as how you might express one of your talents so the Divine emanates through you. Look at whatever stands in the way of your painting, poetry, dancing, or whatever your gift, and *feel* the feelings associated with that block. While feeling them, be aware of how you feel about releasing the blockage. Go deep with this until you reach a strong feeling within you that your Divine talents *must* be expressed. This creates the energy for the sacrifice of whatever it is that stands in the way. The sacrifice might involve things your parents used to tell you, such as, "You'll never make a living doing that!" Or it could be letting go of the influence of the news media in its negativity and hopelessness. It could be your memory of a series of events when you tried to express your special capability and were rebuffed by others or judged by yourself. Remember that *then* is not *now*.

You can deepen this exercise by reviewing the times you "sacrificed" important things in your life within the context of false sacrifice—those times you felt like a martyr. Imagine the situation again, only this time, redo the sacrifice in an authentic way, one that will free you through the joy of release.

—⇒◆⇐—

In the Arthurian tale of Parsival, the questions "What ails thee?" and "How does this serve?" reveal the true meaning of the grail. The first question demands the sacrifice of whatever stands in the way of feeling compassion. The second question requires a sincere desire to learn what the situation has to teach, and being willing to relinquish self-obsession.

If we are dealing with a personal challenge, we must first ask with compassion what ails us. What is the thing that feels sick within us? Have we hurt someone in a way that prevents us from resolving the issue within? Have we been ignoring our own well-being, not taking good care of the temple of our body? Have we rejected our feeling nature to the degree that we feel unbalanced and rough around the edges due to the walls we've built around us? "What ails thee?" defines the illnesses of the human spirit so the Soul can have direct influence and interaction in our life.

In asking how a situation serves us, we must set aside preconditioned thinking, cherished beliefs, and defensive attitudes as the cause of our suffering. When we are willing to sincerely learn how a situation serves, the ego-protector may rebel, but having gone through the many levels of alchemical transformation, we will learn from it rather than be a casualty of it.

With the experience that Distillation and Coagulation give us, we can understand how important these two questions are, whether we ask them about a personal situation or for someone else. In the earlier stages of alchemical transformation, the heart may not be opened yet, so we may lack the mature compassion needed to truly care about what ails someone. The same is true for the second question, because service is generally not a conscious part of the beginning stages. Both of these questions require development of a spiritual maturity that is most powerful during Distillation and Coagulation.

Even though Coagulation is the final stage, the end is just the beginning. This is never a resting place in transformative work, for it requires more from us than ever before and more discomfort if we slip off the pathway than when we were at lesser degrees of unconsciousness.

Few people reach a point of complete, authentic Coagulation and full embodiment of the Philosopher's Stone. Most of us must continue to go through all the stages again and again, each time further refining the golden essence within us. Just as it takes miners time, effort, and toil to uncover riches within the earth, our struggles to find our inner gold are difficult, time-consuming, mettle-testing, and forged in our willingness to sacrifice unconditionally whatever stands in the way.

It takes time to become fully awakened, and the pathway is certainly not glamorous. Those who seek enlightenment are often disappointed when they discover that authentic, deep spirituality has no goal other than the clear perception of one's true nature. Through experiencing that truth, we know that everything about us, as well as everything in our world, is perfect. Everything is exactly as it needs to be in every given moment. The seventh alchemical arcanum says: "The stone is a purified consciousness that remains intact on all levels of reality." This tells us that all of the blocks and limitations of the early stages—Calcination, Dissolution, Separation—have been successfully transformed, and the energy that they previously stored and used to our disadvantage is now freed for us to use creatively, inspirationally, and heartfully. The following meditation is a metaphor for this coagulated state of consciousness, where you now have access to the various levels of your newly transformed consciousness.

COAGULATION MEDITATION: THE GOLDEN TOWER

Relax in a comfortable spot, perhaps while playing quiet music, and close your eyes. Breathe and release yourself into the peace of the meditation.

Imagine a tall, imposing golden tower in front of you. Enter and ascend the spiral stairs. Climb, level after level, until you reach the top. Walk outside to the top level, a turret where you can see 360 degrees around you.

You see a large golden bird flying toward the tower. You sense the air moving under the bird's wings. Suddenly, you are swept onto the bird's back and lifted into the clear blue sky. The bird takes you to a holy place high in the sky where there are seven angels. Sit with them in silence. Enjoy their presence. As you sit with the angels, you notice an incredibly beautiful feminine being, radiating light and holding an exquisite chalice. Standing next to her is a tall man, glowing with light. He holds a golden sword, pointed toward the sky. They welcome you and tell you that the chalice holds all that you are and ever will be, and the sword is your innate power that comes directly from the Divine. They bid you to kneel in front of them, and together, they place a crown on your head. This is the crowning celebration of your coagulated consciousness.

The angels celebrate who you are and tell you how they have guided you since you were created. Each angel touches you, and you can feel the energy flowing into you. Stay with this for as long as you wish.

The Divine Feminine and Masculine beings bless you and release you to return. They remind you of how important it is to continue to remember and practice all that you have learned in the seven stages.

Thank the man and woman and the angels, and climb onto the bird's back for your return to the tower. Descend the tower stairs and reenter your ordinary reality. Write your experiences in your journal.

———⟫•⟪———

In the next chapter on actualizing the results of having worked within the alchemical model of transformation, I present an example of one of the more life-changing events that helped me integrate all the other levels that would introduce me to the experience of Coagulation, where body and spirit become one singular essence, made from the same Divine matter. The alchemists' metaphor for this process is the Phoenix bird, rising from the ashes. The process I'll share with you included the burning and processing in all the seven stages, and it was the only way I would begin to see the possibility of developing my own Coagulation. In the chapter, I will show you how we build our spiritual, mental, and emotional strengths so we have the courage to continue on the pathway to our Philosopher's Stone and redeem our inner gold. After I share my personal experience, I break it down into the results I experienced after going through the event. I also present a more universal picture of how you can apply the seven stages of alchemical transformation to your own processes.

Summary Points

- A coagulated person is a complete, whole being whose consciousness on all levels, whether physical, mental, or emotional, is spiritually integrated. The person has discovered the Philosopher's Stone, which is proof of the work done to completion. The coagulated person perceives life very differently than do ordinary people—he or she lives in a reality where reactivity and fear have been replaced by unified consciousness with the Divine.

- Here again are the alchemical stages we go through: *Calcination:* incinerating the ego's control; *Dissolution:* redeeming emotion and intuition; *Separation:* discovering discernment and wisdom; *Conjunction:* opening the heart through balancing the masculine and the feminine; *Putrefaction-Fermentation:* integrating the lower levels of consciousness with the higher through fire and ferment; *Distillation:* distilling all the work already done and developed to a pure essence; and *Coagulation:* the total surrender into a new consciousness of wholeness.

- In all the levels, some degree of sacrifice is required; the ego's desires, protections, and controls are relinquished for the greater good.

- A coagulated person no longer projects disowned parts of self onto others; we see others as mirrors for ourselves to learn from, not as a judgment of self.

- Each coagulated, conscious person contributes to the healing of the collective consciousness. They know that everything they do, say, think, and feel affects the entire globe and universe.

- Wise, coagulated people contribute in many ways to healing others, but also know when not to help out or rescue—this is so the person may learn the lesson he or she is being given without interruption.

• Living a coagulated life involves living by many spiritual truths, including these two questions: "What ails thee?"—meaning moving out of our own perception and being authentically compassionate to another; and "How does this serve?"—which requires a determination to understand and being willing to relinquish defenses and self-obsessions. Knowing the true answers to these questions reveals a matured and evolved consciousness.

• Again, we must experience Coagulation over and over, just like with the other stages. This long pathway of repetition may cause some to give up and turn away. But the ones who stick with it finally discover the meaning of the Philosopher's Stone—that our goal has never been anything other than authentic perception of one's true nature and connection with the Divine. Through this, we learn that everything is exactly perfect in every given moment.

CHAPTER 14

ACTUALIZED
ALCHEMY

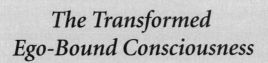

*The Transformed
Ego-Bound Consciousness*

Earlier in this book, I introduced you to my life's major challenge: the conflict between ego inflation and deep feelings of inadequacy. Now, since you have read the book, done the exercises and meditations, and have a grasp on how to apply the concepts and suggestions, you'll understand more about how working alchemically with our issues can transform our lives. My purpose in sharing my process with you is to help you strengthen your belief that you, too, can transform your deep issues, especially when you are immersed in your own "dark night of the Soul."

Though this next segment may seem to suggest that my issue was transformed practically overnight, please keep in mind all of the other material I shared with you about how I worked with this particular challenge throughout each stage of my life. It took *all* of those experiences, many times repeated, until I embodied the full change of consciousness. It also required a great amount of tenacity to keep surrendering to my alchemical dismemberment so I could be put together again consciously—this is Coagulation. Going through the fire of Calcination took me a long time because my ego kept fighting loss of control. But I would bounce back and forth between it and Dissolution, where I could deepen my awareness of and relationship to my emotions. The Separation stage allowed me to review what I'd been through but with more understanding since it is a mental level, though not what I would call "intellectual"—more like learning to think more intuitively and include my emotions in the process. Then, being drawn into the Putrefaction-Fermentation stage of consciousness served as a potent catalyst that would reveal my deepest fears and resistances. I found this stage to be frightening but fascinating at the same time. While in it, I believe I was already sensing the gifts I would discover in Distillation as I became more aware of my authentic self. When I finally was able to move closer into Coagulation, it was only because I had been dragged back into Putrefaction-Fermentation by a profoundly ego-demolishing event. This is referred to in alchemy as the *mortificadio*, where we are once again, as in the first stages, boiled down to our essence, but to a much more conscious and potent degree. Being *mortified* extracts power from the ego's control. It is a death process of laying the previous role of the ego to rest. As the catalyst was added to my process, the ego was wrung into obedience by my higher Self, and this pushed me further, higher, deeper into the inner conjuncted Sacred Marriage with Spirit that I'd always desired. But don't get me wrong! This was not some romanticized spiritual experience. It was one of the roughest yet most rewarding highlights of my life.

The entry into my *mortificadio* was foreshadowed by a vulnerability pact I made with myself one day. I wanted to open myself to all experience without allowing the ego to defend me in its habitual ways. In a way, it was like another Calcination, only this time, I was far more conscious as I battled the ego in the fire—this time I knew why I had to be purified by fire. I wanted to see and feel what life would be like without the armoring of the ego. Here was my opportunity to apply Dissolution consciously by opening myself to my true feelings. My determination to address the ego face on, combined with the pact, reduced the power of the old defenses and protections. This let me experience authentic and pure vulnerability. To consciously release my protection was an act of sacrifice, which is always required for authentic transformation to take place. Through sacrificing what we'd always believed was safety, we let go of old concretized beliefs, attitudes, and energies for ones that are new, heightened, and expanded into heretofore-unrealized realms of consciousness.

Long before I made my vulnerability pact, I had been exploring for years what the ego inflation–inadequacy issue meant in my life. Once I sensed that my core strength was adequate, I made the agreement with myself to experiment with being vulnerable for a week—just a week—so that I could consciously *feel* into this experience that the ego-protector had always guarded me from. I wanted to test it, taste it, and experience how it might have made me feel as a child before the ego inflation's protection was solidly in place. I also wanted to feel it in present time so that

I could compare the feelings of vulnerability within the two periods in my life—one very unconsciously when I was a child, and the other in present time with a greater, more conscious awareness.

I slowed down my usual daily pace so that I could pay attention to the feeling of vulnerability. I went about my ordinary business, going to the market, fueling my car, teaching classes, seeing counselees, and talking with family and friends. I was aware of how strange it was not to feel my usual defenses. It felt rather gentle, soft, pleasing—and relieving. I felt a great weight had been lifted from me.

Only a few days into the experiment, I was oblivious that my self-chosen state of vulnerability and defenselessness was leading me to the edge of a new boundary of consciousness. Here, I would be catapulted through this at a speed eclipsing any conscious agreement, and dumped into my unconscious self to experience it from an open and new perspective. When the catalyst for this experience began, it felt like the old, familiar Putrefaction, but it went much deeper than any previous experiences in this level. It was only after the entire experience had played itself out that I could begin to understand that my life's core issue—the battle between arrogance and inadequacy—had been transformed. It was clear that it was the purpose of it all, from the moment I intuitively created the experience of vulnerability to the resolution at the end of the *mortificadio*. When our ego's protection of inflation—in my case, arrogance—is stripped bare and disempowered so it can no longer compensate for the opposite and underlying belief in inadequacy, it becomes a death of the outdated and a rebirth of our relationship to Soul. The experience of death is always required in an authentic alchemical process. Without dying to what has held us back through undergoing a *mortificadio* experience, we will continue to experience our main issue over and over until we are willing to surrender to the transformative death experience.

A few weeks prior to my vulnerability pact, I'd been working on the question of arrogance and other ways the ego inflated to protect me, consciously keeping it in mind as I related to others, making sure it didn't leak out and hurt people as it had in the past. I knew better than to try to "get rid of it," so I was working with its energy in meditation and the various processes I've shared in this book to transform the energy of it. Carrying the embodied results of all the inner work I'd been doing, along with my new vulnerability, I ventured out one day…

On this particular day, as I drove along in my car, enjoying a sense of freedom from my old inflations, I saw a woman I knew going the opposite direction. I hailed her with a wave and stopped the car to smile and greet her, but was shocked to be met with a face of sheer rage. She began to rail at me, accusing me of things I hadn't actually done, and when I tried to calm the situation and investigate what had really happened, I was met with more rage, an insult, and a dismissive gesture as she drove away.

I was shaken to my core. I felt parts of me grasping for any of my old protections to save me. But they had not risen to my defense because I had vowed to set them aside. Devastated, I went home crying and feeling humiliated (humiliation is what *mortificadio* is all about!). Though I knew that the woman was projecting her own old, unresolved rage onto me, it still didn't soften the impact. My heart felt as if it had been shot with arrows.

Over the next couple days, I tried to pull myself back to my center but found it profoundly difficult. I couldn't shake the heavy sensations in my body. My emotions didn't feel like my own. I sensed that I'd "eaten" her rage, and it was now stuck in my body. I had jumped naively into what I thought vulnerability would be, but had neglected my boundaries, which are positive and life-affirming protections that are not functions of the ego-protector. Rather, they serve us as wise, mature safeguards against unhealthy energies that throw us off balance and pull us off purpose.

So much for being vulnerable, I thought. Still, I knew this had happened for a purpose, especially since I'd consciously agreed to be vulnerable. I did some energy clearing with the help of a healer, and continued meditating and praying for the highest resolution for both the angry woman and myself. I also worked in the Separation stage so I could dissect the whole experience to see what I'd learned from it. I knew that my arrogance in past interactions with her had most likely come to a head now, so I asked myself how this difficult situation was serving me to further transform the old behavior. I found it intriguing that while I had been haughty with her in the past, for me, it had truly become a thing of the past, since I'd been working on this issue diligently for a couple of years before this incident. Consequently, to be accused of still acting in an outdated way seemed bizarre, yet it certainly got my attention. Her rage was the catalyst in the Putrefaction-Fermentation pot that I had needed to transform my life challenge.

What I didn't know then was that this event, combined with my vulnerability pact, would expose the deepest, darkest layers of the ego's realm within me. The inner work I'd done with Brugh and by myself had set me up over many years for this point of ego peril—my confrontation with what had been hidden in deeper realms of consciousness.

For most of my life, I had allowed the ego to rule with an "off with your head" method of resolving difficulties. This was fearsome enough to protect me from many experiences in which my life or well-being may have been, or seemed to be, compromised. It also protected me from experiences I may have wanted to have but didn't follow through on because the ego had trained me to fear stepping out from its protection.

On the third morning after the incident, I tried meditating, but I kept flip-flopping back and forth between inner peace and terrible anxiety over the event. There was a colossal battle going on between my intention to live from my higher self and the ego's desperate bid to regain control. I could not hold my center for more than a few minutes at a time. Finally, I broke down sobbing for a very long time. When the crying subsided, I was weak, numb, and emotionless. It was particularly strange because, unlike my usually active mind, I had no thoughts of any kind. My mind was empty.

Then, without my ego's agreement and before I could stop myself, I found myself leaving my house and heading to the angry woman's home. It felt as if something else were moving me. I was definitely *not* in control. My mind and emotions were so deadened, I couldn't fight this physical movement toward what I assumed would be a disaster.

As I knocked on my adversary's door, I didn't know what I was going to say. When she opened the door and cautiously invited me inside, I felt like I was going into a lion's den and that my very existence was on the line. I opened my mouth to speak but could only manage to say, "I ..." before I burst into sobs again. I was stunned when she reached out and held me for the entire time I cried. My entire body began to shake violently from head to toe. (This is an experience called a *kriya*, in which previously blocked energies burst forth to be released, healed, and transformed.) Though it felt very strange, the shaking also felt like a relief, which of course it was. My "beach ball" theory was playing itself out—my body was releasing years of the ego's restrictive protection.

As my shaking and sobs began to subside, the woman invited me to sit and gave me a glass of water. For a very long time, I tried to find words but couldn't. She just sat quietly waiting until I could.

When I finally spoke, still shaking, what tumbled out was very different from anything I'd ever said to anyone. I found myself witnessing a voice within that had been protected by the ego all my life. This new voice clearly stated my innocence in what I'd been accused of. I made a strong statement that never again would I allow myself to be treated like that by her or anyone else. I was surprised that I could say this without criticizing the woman. My words rang so true that I could feel a shift in the energy in the room. This was the Distillation aspect of the experience because it ultimately washed clean so much of my relationship with my ego. I went on to expose to her all my feelings about what had happened. This laying-bare process led me to experience how my arrogance had affected my life and the lives of others, including hers. What I didn't know then, but which became crystal-clear some months later, was that the transformation of my arrogance would open the door to my authentic self. It had lain hidden, slumbering, until I was ready to release my fear-based ego protection of arrogance and move into the kind of majestic perception of life that is associated with the Divine kingdom, rather than the ego's version of superiority.

I made amends to her for my behaviors of the past. I was aware of energy shifts occurring between us, so I used this energy to lay a new groundwork for what was acceptable between us from that time forward. This new voice was strong, clear, and firm, while at the same time compassionate and understanding of the person's painful early life experiences. I sensed that we were both being given a profound opportunity to make necessary changes in our lives. Later, I realized that this new me had been brought to the entry of Distillation by having gone through all the early stages very quickly during the days that this experience was taking place.

This catalyzing experience with the woman's rage also felt like a dismemberment, which represents the breaking up, or dissolution, of old, outdated, and no longer necessary defenses. My *mortificadio* became a death of the inflated ego because it was a *mortification*— the humiliation I felt at having been yelled at in the street. The word *humility* is derived from the word *humus,* a compost made of rotting material. When I was humiliated and the person's arrows of rage struck home, my inflated ego burst and spilled out all of its putrefied contents, which could now be fermented as powerful fertilizer for a more conscious life. As strange as it may seem, I will always be grateful to her for the experience that broke me loose and offered me freedom. I believe that gratitude to those who hurt us by asking how it serves brings us closer to our authentic and golden self.

In hopes of further invigorating and encouraging you in your own transformative processes, I share here some of the results that occurred not long after I was able to clearly process this event. This does not imply a formula that fits everyone, but you may experience something similar. You'll know when authentic change has occurred because you'll feel far more loving toward yourself and less likely to criticize yourself. You'll feel a deep change within that you may have never known, or perhaps forgotten. The change consists of your having transformed the aspects of yourself that held you down—like lead—and now you can celebrate having discovered the gold that has been in you all along!

- First, I knew intuitively that this had been an authentic transformation, not just wishful thinking. I knew a substantial change had occurred because of the way I felt about myself now—it was a new relationship, one full of creativity, joy, and serenity. This was a Conjunction-level experience, a sacred marriage of all the wonderful, golden parts of me having come together in an inner community.

- I began to feel far more grounded and human because I was not being directed by my ego, which had always made me believe that I wasn't part of this earth because I was superior and above it all. By being "humus-ified," for the first time in my life I surrendered to being human and embraced my connection to the earth. This is an experience that results from the Fermentation level—the catalyst, like the one that vintners add at a certain point in winemaking to perfect the wine, can be anything that shakes us to our core to help us release all that is outdated, outsized, and outgrown.

- I continued to stay vulnerable but with wise, sensible boundaries. I was able to do this by working within the principles of Separation, where we discern what we want to keep in our lives and what we can now release.

- My emotions became more clear and present, and I feel them now more keenly and consciously than ever. (Have you ever had the experience of not knowing what you felt about a situation until much later?) I am now able to come within reach of what I'm feeling in the moment because the old defenses are no longer present. I no longer dread that my feelings will annihilate me. The Dissolution level of alchemy plunges us into our emotions, offering us the opportunity to really feel them authentically, sometimes for the first time.

- I became able to be direct without offending or worrying about what others will think of me. This new maturity was a result of having gone through the Putrefaction-Fermentation levels since they were potent enough to help me grow past my old concerns about others' perceptions of me. It was a maturation process, that when combined with what I had learned in Conjunction about opening my heart, I could let go of another's opinions and love the person anyway.

- My energy levels have changed. Holding that "beach ball" down for so long had been devouring my energy!

- I feel an at-one-ment, a unity, a kinship, with myself and with others. This was impossible while the ego-protector was in control. The inflated ego divides, conquers, and convinces us that separation is a fact. This is how we can feel when we touch into the Coagulation level. We feel no separation between us and anything else in the universe—it is a sign that our consciousness is becoming unified with everything designed and created by the Divine.

- For some months after the experience, I felt turned inside out. I began to recall and appreciate who I was at the very beginning of my existence in this life and before. I discovered my powerful feminine force that guided, rather than controlled, as the ego-protector had done. I found the inner feminine to be healing, compassionate, and strong. Throughout the experience and long after, I depended upon the Separation level to help me understand the more subtle and invaluable gifts I'd been given in my *mortificadio*.

If there is such a thing as a "secret formula" in spiritual development, it consists of opening up to conscious awareness of each and every experience. Personally, this formed a strong foundation for my vulnerability agreement, the sacrifice of my defenses. My work in alchemical transformation over the years had created a firm foundation so that the purpose of my *mortificadio* experience was clearly to accept the transmutation of arrogance into compassion, wholeness, and right use of power.

Your issues and challenges are unique to you, so your process will be different than mine. But the bones of what I experienced seem to be universal:

1. A catalyst appears at some point before or around the time of our physical birth that will open the door to the main life challenge our Souls have chosen. My catalyst was being born a girl, which was not as acceptable in my family than if I'd been a boy. This was the root of my almost lifelong experience of rejection. Examples of other catalysts include being born into a household of addiction or abuse, being born with a physical affliction, or losing parents at an early age.

2. In our early life, the ego protects us from vulnerability to the catalyst's powerful influence on our feelings. This is crucial to our being able to stay connected to our Souls and to learn how to deal with life issues ignited by the catalyst.

3. Conflict between ego-protection and feelings about ourselves creates the major life issue that springs forth from the initial catalyst. This is the issue that we will spend much of our lives working to resolve. We may also have a deep sense, which we may not be consciously aware of, that our Soul has a purpose for our life. The frustration this leads to adds impact and motivation in resolving the life issue. This is the time that we either consciously agree to work on our issue in Calcination, or life insists upon giving us the opportunity.

4. Eventually, the conflict reaches a saturation point, which wakes us to how the ego's protection no longer serves, yet its control persists. Many times this is introduced by a crisis of some kind in our lives, from which we cannot escape if we try to use the ego's old protections. This is when the fire of Calcination begins to heat up and we can't get away from the problem. We can choose to feel victimized or to work *with* the process, bringing ourselves into further deepening our alchemical work.

5. Either through the pain of crisis or existential insight, we may be motivated to intensify the deep inner work of Calcination. This requires the sacrifice—the burning up—of old, cherished beliefs and attitudes and a surrender into defenselessness and vulnerability, which is the preamble to embracing the attributes

of heart-level consciousness. (Note: Not everyone would be interested in what I did with vulnerability. We need our protections until we have a strong-enough core to transform them. Doing the other exercises in this book can take you far in your transformative work—I do not recommend the vulnerability experience for anyone who feels it is not for them or it is not time for them to engage with it.)

6. The crisis point forces us to either step fully into the work or accept an unfinished life. By choosing to face the crisis, we gain the opportunity to learn from the unconscious in a conscious way. My crisis point was the attack in the street by the woman. Yours may be loss of an important career or loved one, or perhaps a health crisis. This is the Dissolution level, where our emotions begin to express strongly and it may seem like you are out of control as you cry, rage, or grieve.

7. The power of Dissolution takes us into Separation, where we review what has happened. If we can sincerely answer the two potent questions "What ails thee?" and "How does this serve?," we will be able to move closer to our Souls.

8. Emerging from what we experienced in the unconscious, we forge a strong, new perception of ourselves that is in alignment with the Soul and its purpose. Here is the *hieros gamos*, the Sacred Marriage, or the Conjunction of your human essence with your Soul. Energetically, it's as if a flash of light enters you to ignite this relationship, preparing you for whatever is next in your process of unwinding and deepening your understanding of your life issue.

9. In the level of Putrefaction-Fermentation, potent forces begin to rip and strip away the old, habitual ways that kept us from freedom, and forcing us into consciousness. This occurred to me when I began to cry and shake, then made amends, and finally determined how I would protect myself consciously from then on, rather than allowing the ego-protector to employ its outdated devices.

10. Now we begin to experience life differently. We perceive others in ways we never could before while the ego's criticisms were active. And we perceive ourselves as feeling "real," like our true selves. In this stage of Distillation it's as if we are climbing out of a deep well into a new world filled with new potential for supporting who we've always dreamed of becoming. We can feel the golden self very present within—and can celebrate it.

11. Our life issue is transformed by new strength. We are freed to reveal and share our authentic, coagulated selves, and we begin to live life according to our Soul's direction. In alchemy, this is the revelation of the Philosopher's Stone: the gold within us.

I suspect that, because life is cyclical, there will always be cracks between life stages and growth mysteries that require additional previously unimaginable inner work. I also suspect that the answer to this dilemma is just as challenging: Keep going—never give up!

Authentic spiritual transformation requires the willingness to risk old beliefs, preconditions, and projections onto others. There is nothing holding you back from the full recall of your greater consciousness but your perceptions of yourself.

Wholeness is inexorably linked to holiness, and, interestingly, the word *holy* has its roots in *hale*, which means "sound, whole, and happy." In the alchemical model of spiritual transformation, a holy person is one who has gone through all the lower stages: Calcination, where we burn out the ego's control; Dissolution, where we discover hidden feelings and learn how to use them to advantage; Separation, where we learn how to discern what's important; and then explore Conjunction to seek balance and the gifts of one's heart. After this basic work is solidly integrated, we are free to choose whether or not to proceed into the exacting stages of Putrefaction-Fermentation, where we experience wrestling matches with the more potent of our inner challenges; Distillation, where we become far more interested in the greater good than merely our own; and finally Coagulation, where true wholeness-holiness is revealed. Few wish to move on to the higher realms of alchemical work since they are so powerful and exacting. However, the end is just the beginning. For as we have strengthened ourselves in all ways and moved into the realizational state of consciousness, we also move into more responsibility to ourselves and our growth as well as to others and all of life itself. This is no resting place, other than on deep inner levels, ones that are based in trusting the process. It requires more responsiveness than ever before, possibly more discomfort and pain than when we were working in the lower levels, and more vision of how our moment-to-moment decisions can affect entire universes. This work is also filled with many moments of joy and expansive understanding and perception of life that we never experienced before.

Few people reach the point of *complete* Coagulation. Most of us must continue to go through all of the stages again and again, each time further refining the golden essence within us. It takes time to become fully awakened. If we are pursuing a fervent goal to become enlightened, we may actually prevent ourselves from achieving it, for true spirituality has no goal other than to remember one's true nature. In the moments of experiencing that truth, we know that everything about us and everything in our world is perfect—not in the usually accepted definition of perfection, because that's impossible, but everything is exactly as it needs to be in every given moment.

I hope this book has offered you new ways of changing inaccurate perceptions of yourself by transforming judgment and self-criticism as blocks to self-awareness, discovering your Soul's purpose by using the steps within transformational alchemy, and opening your heart. True Alchemy of the Soul helps us make this shift from constantly finding fault with ourselves to finding the gold within us.

Now that you've moved through the seven stages of transformational alchemy and experienced the exercises and meditations, you might want to try the process in Appendix A: The Gold Within You Process. It will help you to clarify anything you were not sure of as you worked through the stages. It will also give you a better idea of how the ego has played its role in your life.

Summary Points

- This chapter showed you the results of my having worked within the alchemical model to transform my life's major challenge: the conflict between ego inflation and deep feelings of inadequacy. It is an example of one of the more life-changing events that helped me integrate all the other levels that would introduce me to the experience of Coagulation, where body and spirit become one singular essence, made from the same Divine matter.

- I showed you how we build our spiritual, mental, and emotional strengths so we have the courage to continue on the pathway to our Philosopher's Stone and redeem our inner gold. I also broke down the results I experienced after going through the event, and presented a more universal model that you can apply using the seven stages of alchemical transformation in your own processes.

ℰ𝒜PPENDIX A
The Gold Within You Process:
The Way to the Philosopher's Stone

The Gold Within You process emerged organically during one of the periods many years ago of working with my major life issue of ego inflation and inadequacy. I sensed it would work well for me since it employed both left-brain and right-brain resources (logic and intuition). In this system, I recognized an opportunity to apply principles of transformational alchemy to all I was exploring. I began to test it in my workshops and was amazed and delighted that students reported that previously insurmountable issues responded dramatically to the Gold Within You process with authentic and long-lasting results.

In the Gold Within You process, an essential key is the embodiment of adversity as an ally for growth. By not rejecting it in an attempt to "get rid of it," adversity has the power to induce profound insight and change. The steps in the Gold Within You process are very similar to how the alchemist makes pure gold from lead. Whether we are a laboratory alchemist or a person wishing to transform consciousness, the process is the same: through metamorphoses of old material, we observe the resultant transformations (both difficult and Divine), and the gold (within the glass beaker or within ourselves) is revealed in its shining state.

The Gold Within You process will help you develop a new response to difficult or unacceptable experiences. Rather than rejecting the unacceptable, you will learn to embrace the wisdom within the experience while releasing belief in negative interpretations of aspects of self. It doesn't matter what we wish to transform—compulsive behavior, shyness, feelings of inadequacy, addictive behaviors, creative blocks, or depression—this process reveals an alternative way to perceive adversity as a catalyst for genuine healing. The task is not in getting the problem to change, but rather in changing our perception of it.

The Gold Within You process is simple and easy to utilize, because it begins by drawing information from the intellect, where the ego-protector typically resides. The early steps required can "sabotage the saboteur" by outwitting the ego and leading it to releasing its habitual control. (The exercise in Appendix B: Writing a New Job Description for Your Ego-Protector may also assist you in this.)

The Gold Within You process helps you to redeem emotions that were frozen by fear in the past. This allows emotion to circulate freely, as it does naturally when blocks to its expression are transformed.

As the first stage of the Gold Within You employs your intellect, you will learn to clearly identify and define the problem to be solved. In the second stage you will move deeper into the roots of the issue and learn about what triggers it. The third stage consists of defining what defends you from wanting to resolve the issue. The final stage of the process involves the development of new perceptions of adversity.

The Gold Within You Process

Stage One: Getting Started

We'll begin the Gold Within You process by consciously engaging the left hemisphere of the brain, which will assist in identifying and defining the problem to be solved. Our purpose in doing so is to feed the left brain information that will ultimately serve to disengage it from the control of the ego and the limited perceptions upon which beliefs are built. The ego feels most comfortable when the left brain, or rational aspects of our minds, are given a task. So in this step we will actually be employing the ego to loosen its control over your life by drawing its attention away from its usual job of protection.

The ego's fears of annihilation or loss of control are pacified by words and ideas. As the ego is calmed, the emotional-intuitive aspects are freed to move onstage to explore and transform the underlying beliefs that support the problem.

Stage One—Step 1

The best place to start is to look at your greatest challenge. If there are multiple challenges, that's fine, too. Begin by writing them down in list form with a title, as shown in the example below.

In the days that follow, write down anything that seems or feels important about any of the items on your list, no matter how silly or trivial it might seem. In the example, these thoughts are in parentheses. Keep your list available so it's easy to add things as you think of them. (Hint: Not editing is a very important part of this process! From free-flowing and unexpected material we receive keys to the secrets within us.)

Example: Current Challenges

1. **Fights with my significant other.** (I'm angry when s/he puts me down; I feel like nothing; I get confused as to who is right.)

2. **Frustration in my job.** (Everyone else on staff seems to be getting ahead, but I don't seem to be noticed. I was passed over for a recent raise and it made me feel rotten about myself.)

3. **Vague, upsetting, unpleasant feelings.** (I have to be busy all the time or I'll lose control and fall apart. Sometimes my feelings get me in trouble with others; they think I'm too emotional. I've tried to be a good person, but nothing good ever happens to me. I feel like there's something really wrong with me.)

As you review your list, look at what the words are telling you, and feel deeply into what you have written. What can you discern about these issues? Most importantly, how are they all similar? In the example thus far, it could be that they all fall in the category of not feeling good about or believing in yourself.

Stage One—Step 2

Give your list a title. From the previous example, we can easily see an underlying issue of negative beliefs, attitudes, or perceptions. So the title might be something like this:

Not Feeling Good About Myself

Stage One—Step 3

Now your task is to make a list of all the words and brief phrases that might describe the issue. This step helps to bring more awareness of how you feel about or experience the issue. It also creates a foundation for the next steps. (Hint: Remember not to edit! Just write things down as they come to you, even if they don't make sense.) Using the example, we might make a list that looks like this:

Not Feeling Good About Myself

How I'd Describe This:

- not good enough • lazy • unsuccessful • stupid • useless
- angry • irritated • unmotivated • unnoticed • insignificant
- too emotional • immature • out of touch • inadequate
- bossy • pushy • low self-esteem • scared • valueless
- disrespected • unhappy • sad

Next, using a dictionary and a thesaurus, look up each word and write down any words you find that feel connected to the key word, especially if it has a "charge" in it. (Hint: Words that carry a "feeling," or a personal emotional charge, can provide you with clues that will help in your understanding of the issue.) Also, many of your words may reoccur. These are the ones to pay particular attention to because they are the building blocks of the underlying belief. Notice which words in the list repeat often; these are the clue words. You may want to circle these particularly powerful words or mark them with a highlighter.

Your list may look something like this, though I have abbreviated it with just a few of the words and their synonyms. Yours will be longer and more detailed.

Not Feeling Good About Myself

Words That Describe My Issue:

- **not good** (unsatisfactory, inadequate, unacceptable, insufficient, ineffective, not enough)
- **lazy** (unwilling to work, idle, shiftless, malingering)
- **unsuccessful** (a failure, a loser, useless, unlucky, doomed)
- **stupid** (not intelligent, dumb, witless, retarded, dense, ignorant, mindless)
- **useless** (worthless, of no use, ineffective, unproductive, futile)
- **angry** (mad, enraged, pissed off, irritated, bitter)
- **irritated** (annoyed, angry, disturbed, exasperated, hurt, gets on my nerves)
- **unmotivated** (uninspired, apathetic, lazy, goal-less)
- **unnoticed** (ignored, disregarded, discounted, not being paid attention to, unrecognized)
- **insignificant** (inconsequential, unimportant, trivial, meaningless, useless, not worth mentioning)
- **too emotional** (overly sensitive, over-reactive, temperamental, disturbing)
- **immature** (undeveloped, incomplete, imperfect, infantile, childish, inexperienced)

Review of Stage One

Step 1: Identify the challenge. Review your list daily, adding important ideas, thoughts, feelings, and intuitions.

Step 2: Give your challenge a title.

Step 3: Make a list of descriptive words about the challenge, using a dictionary and thesaurus to find other related descriptive words.

Identify by circling or marking with an asterisk those words or phrases that hold a particular charge or repeat themselves.

Stage Two: Deep Roots and Triggers

In this stage, you'll move deeper into the roots of the issue. The first step in Stage Two involves making another list, but this time it contains events that trigger the issue. This step increases our awareness of the issue and what catalyzes it. It helps us to recognize the outer and inner influences that trigger the issue as a whole, but also contribute to the way we react to it.

Stage Two—Step 1

In this step, the title you've previously given the issue may change and become more accurate. The title of the example we were using was "Not Feeling Good About Myself." It may be more accurate now to change that title to "Negative Self-Regard."

Now the list might look something like this:

Negative Self-Regard

What Triggers It:

I tend to feel bad/depressed/angry/etc., about myself when:

- someone betrays me • someone insults me
- I don't get what I want • I have financial problems
- someone chooses another over me • I fail at something
- I don't know what to do • I'm criticized
- I'm left out • I feel unworthy • I feel vulnerable

Keep your list with you throughout your week and keep adding to it as you think of more catalysts.

Stage Two—Step 2

Just as you did in Stage One, the second step in Stage Two is to look at each item on your list and observe the emotion contained within the trigger. Your purpose is neither to amplify the feeling nor to act upon it, but just to feel it enough so that you can identify what happens when your issue is triggered. (Hint: Emotions can sometimes be more easily accessed through bodily sensations. If you have trouble discovering an emotion, focus on what your body is doing at the moment, then put that feeling on your list. That feeling will relate to an emotion even if you're not immediately aware of which one. For example, if your stomach cramps up, you're probably dealing with fear. If you're feeling dizzy, you may be experiencing an underlying confusion, usually covering another feeling, perhaps fear of change.)

Here is an example of the feelings that might be related to the triggers listed in step 1:

Negative Self-Regard

Ways It Manifests:

When triggered, my issue expresses itself in these ways:

- When someone betrays me, I feel angry, shaky, insecure, lost, distrusting of people, distrusting of life, judgmental toward the one betraying me, or I shut the person out of my life.

- When someone insults me, I feel hurt and small, like I want to cry, to withdraw, to insult them back, or to defend myself but don't know how. I question whether the person was actually right about me, become officious or bossy, or feel the need to prove myself.

- When I don't get what I want, I become angry, pout, manipulate a way to get it anyway, or believe I'll never get it.

- When I have financial problems, I worry, fear destitution and homelessness, or believe I don't really deserve anything anyway.

- When someone chooses another over me, I feel jealous, hurt, lost, undeserving, or like I want to withdraw.

- When I fail at something, I feel depressed, unworthy, powerless, or like I'll never succeed.

- When I don't know what to do, I feel confused or angry at being confused, or I want to give up.

- When I'm criticized, I feel angry, retributive, sad, or despairing, or I believe that my Inner Critic is right.
- When I'm left out, I feel rejected, abandoned, angry at the unfairness of it, like I'm rejectable because I'm so unworthy, bad, different, etc.
- When I feel unworthy, I feel like I'm nothing and not important, like I'm just taking up space in the world.
- When I feel vulnerable, I feel fearful, unprotected, small, like I am powerless.

Review of Stage Two

Step 1: Make a list of things that trigger the challenge.

Step 2: Identify the emotions related to each trigger. Learn how each catalyst manifests in your life.

Stage Three: Defense Against the Challenge

The third stage involves defining what defends you from being willing to deal with the challenge.

Stage Three—Step 1

The title of this list might be:

My Defenses

The key to making a list of defenses is to first imagine feeling the feelings described in Stage Two, step 2, and then imagining one of the actions you tend to take to deny, hide from, or defend against those feelings.

An example might be: Someone says something rude, so you feel hurt and then you:

a. lash back rudely

b. walk away, feeling like crying

c. withdraw, holding the anger inside

d. project your own feelings about yourself onto the person ("Well, he's just a useless jerk!")

A very helpful way to work with many of these steps is through a process known as *mindmapping*. You can use it to start the Gold Within You process, or whenever you feel stuck about any issue in your life. It will help you focus and bring forth more information from your subconscious.

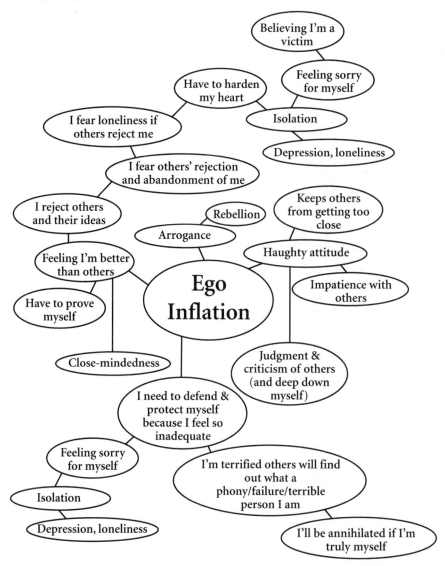

Using a large piece of paper, start by drawing a large circle in the center in which you write the issue you're working with. Then begin connecting smaller circles with words and phrases that come up freely and automatically—don't worry if they don't make sense now. Connect the small circles with the large one or other small ones with lines—do this intuitively. Write as rapidly as you can so the linear, rational thinking mind doesn't have a chance to edit, and you'll discover words and phrases that are more authentic—some of them will surprise you. The example shows how I used my issue of ego inflation and feelings of inadequacy in the mind map. Watch how the lines progress from one circle to the next, moving outward and expanding from the center—this indicates a deepening of awareness about the subject which is revealed by the subconscious.

Stage Three—Step 2

After making a list of your typical defenses, study each one over the next few days until you can identify which underlying beliefs justify the need for each defense. For instance, in the previous example, if someone treats you rudely and you react by withdrawing, your underlying belief might be something like, "I don't deserve to be treated with respect." Or if your reaction was yelling back at the person, your underlying belief might be, "I have to defend myself because I feel my very existence is being threatened." Please make sure you do this step without judging yourself—this is a most important key.

Stage Three—Step 3

What would you guess is *always* the factor underlying the need for defenses? The answer is fear. Our personal defenses serve the same purpose. As you deepen this inner work, keep in mind that your task is to find what fear your defenses are guarding you against feeling. This is most effectively done by accessing the belief that creates the defense.

For instance, if someone has been rude to you, the belief underlying your inner reaction can lead you to what the core fear is. If your belief is that you don't deserve to be treated with respect, the fear may be the belief that you're nothing, that you have no value. If your belief leads you to fight back, then it's possible that the fear beneath your reaction is that of annihilation. In either scenario, you're dealing with the fear of not existing. Isn't this the bottom-line fear we all share, personally and collectively? It causes us to think that anything that feels like an attack against us means we will no longer exist.

This step involves contemplating your relationship to fear and where it plays roles in your life, then identifying the main underlying fear. In this review, you may discover several levels of fear before you reach the one at the bottom of the pile. As I continued to use the Gold Within You process with my own issues, I learned the importance of moving deeper and deeper into the various levels of fear until the essential, primal fear was identified.

Stage Four: Realizations

This last stage involves the realization of how your challenge has ultimately served you.

Stage Four—Step 1

This stage requires taking the time to integrate all you've learned. Do this by meditating, journaling, or talking with a trusted therapist or friend about all that you've learned as a result of the Gold Within You process. The first task is to write a short story or poem about how your challenge has served you. Write in either first or third person (by stepping away from the more personal first person, the ego shows less interest in shutting down the creative process). Use your creativity to write a fantasy, a mystery, a science fiction story, or even a thank-you letter to your Soul—whatever wants to express through you. Put what you've written aside for a few days, then reread it, allowing it to sink deep inside you. This is a time to appreciate how you've redeemed important aspects and energies within you so that you feel more whole, complete, and authentic. This step of storywriting engages the right brain with its intuitive and creative aspects. Without these elements to balance the process and lead to integration through its connection to the Soul, the process would be incomplete.

Stage Four—Step 2

The final step in the Gold Within You process provides a means by which to review the challenge from a higher and deeper perspective, one that does not perceive through the filters of belief in victimization or adversity as a burden, but rather as a gift that teaches and supports us. This is the most important part of this entire process, since it brings us full circle, back to the issue itself, yet with a new, unconditional view of why we experienced it, and why it was such a potent teacher for us.

I've provided my own complete chart here as an example.

THE GOLD WITHIN YOU
My Challenge: Power Drive/Ego Inflation vs. Belief in Inadequacy

Outer Catalysts/Triggers: Betrayal, challenge, insecurity, insult/ offense, rejection, others' successes or acknowledgment, others' beliefs, abandonment, the unknown, having to be responsible, expectations of myself and others.

Manifests as the Following Defenses: Officiousness, arrogance, haughty attitude, entitlement, belief in being better than others, need to prove myself, hardened heart, rejection of others and their ideas, close-mindedness, stubbornness, isolation/distancing, know-it-all attitude, impatience with others (see Sample Defenses Chart that follows), obsessive organizer, manipulator, covering confusion by pretending not to understand, need to know, pouting/feeling sorry for myself (belief in victimization), rebellion, judgment/criticism of self and others, uncooperativeness.

Underlying Belief to Justify Defenses: "I need to defend/protect myself because I feel so inadequate."

Underlying Fear/s: What the defenses are defending me against knowing/feeling/experiencing.

> **First Level:** "I'll never succeed, I'll never be anything or anyone, I'll never be enough, I'll never meet my own or others' expectations."

Second Level: "I'm terrified others will discover what a failure/ phony/terrible person I am."

Bottom Level—The Belief Underlying All Else: "I will be annihilated if I'm truly myself."

You'll find that the second and final levels tend to mirror each other, no matter what the issue or whose chart it is. Underlying all problems, whether individual or global, is fear. So it's important to pay attention to what you discover as the bottom levels—they will always be about fear. If they aren't, you haven't gone deep enough within yourself to discover what lies at the heart of the issue you want to transform. The next exercise, "Sample Defenses Chart," will help you do this.

This is another example that shows how we can complete our first chart and then perhaps decide to go even deeper, especially if we've had a difficult time defining the levels in Stage Four, step 2. In this exercise, we would choose a highly charged word from the original chart and then take it through the steps in the Gold Within You process. Once again, I use my own example here. Notice how the final realization reveals fear as the cause of the issue.

Sample Defenses Chart

Defense: Impatience

Dictionary Definition: Annoyance because of delay, restless eagerness to do something or go somewhere, not being willing to bear or tolerate, showing dislike for.

Synonyms from Thesaurus: Tense, irritated, agitated, fussy, abrupt, rude, disrespectful, anxious, irritable, irascible, brusque, annoyed, touchy, intolerant, narrow-minded, close-minded.

Underlying Belief to Justify This Defense: "Only I can do things properly or well enough because I'm smarter than everyone else."

Underlying Fear/s: (What this protection of impatience is defending against knowing/feeling/experiencing. Once again, note how the bottom levels tend to always be the same or similar to the underlying fears in the main issue.)

First Level: "Others will take over." (Loss of control)

Second Level: "I have to do this quickly or else others will discover what a failure/phony/terrible person I am." (Hit and run)

Bottom Level, Underlying All Else: "If I don't stay in control, I'll be annihilated." (Fear of the unknown, and in this example, impatience would be a way to avoid letting go of control.)

How This Issue Serves Me: Being impatient with others and myself reflects how I separate myself from the truth within each situation. It is a defense that covers my need to do things fast so I don't have to stop and feel anything unpleasant or frightening.

Realization: What I Can Develop: Patience, which is the will or ability to wait or endure without complaining or making a disturbance. Patience gives me self-control and quiet strength, helps me persevere, and helps me bear and grow from hardship and challenge. It teaches me restraint under provocation and eliminates a need for retaliation. It allows me to use my natural talent for gentle humor in approaching seemingly intolerable situations. I can develop composure and imperturbability, inner calm and serenity, cool-headedness and even-temperedness.

By the time you've explored and completed all four stages of the Gold Within You process, you will know much more about how you think, feel, and act. You will discover what has limited and prevented you from perceiving yourself and your challenges clearly and fully. And you will be able to recognize more often what is going on within you when you are faced with a difficult situation. When you are consistently aware of your inner experience, you'll make wiser choices and appreciate yourself more when confronted with life's challenges.

$\mathcal{A}$PPENDIX B
Writing a New Job Description
for Your Ego-Protector

You can design a new job description for any aspect of your life that you sense no longer serves you. You could work with the Inner Child, the Inner Critic, or any other aspect—whatever you sense is not helping you to be a mature, healthy individual. Here are the steps involved in discovering the ego's original protective job as well as transforming that job into one that frees and empowers you. As your Inner Alchemist works with you on this, you will go through the fires of Calcination and Putrefaction-Fermentation, and, if you persevere, you can—and will—discover the gold within you!

Unearthing Your Original Job Description
Before embarking on the journey of writing a new job description, some background material must be collected. The best way to do this is by imagining the original job description given to the ego by you, albeit unconsciously and, in all probability, early in your life. Before writing the new job description, it is essential to become aware of how the ego-protector has been operating, what it has done to protect you, and how its protection most likely doesn't serve you any longer.

So let's begin!

Step 1: The Sphere Meditation
The Sphere Meditation will help you detect the information you will need to do the job description work. (You will find detailed instructions on how to do this meditation in chapter 12.) This meditation

presents you with the opportunity to go back into the filing cabinet of your memory to the time when you first "hired" the ego to create a way to protect you with various defenses. Keep in mind that ego defenses are *always* intended to "protect and serve," like your own inner police force. The ego is not your enemy and can become your ally if shown how to be. Be aware that this process requires patience and persistence because the ego may resist this step, since its job is to protect you from getting too close to the emotions that first shaped the need for defense.

Since the ego's defenses were created from deep within the subconscious, you will most likely not remember when or how the original job was created for the ego-protector. So in this meditation, you will use your imagination to discover what the scenario might have been. Trust this. Leave your Doubter outside the entrance of your sphere so you can change perceptions and learn from them.

Step 2: Original Job Template

From what you learned in your Sphere Meditation, you'll be writing your original, protection-oriented job description, as if writing it at the age when the ego protection was born. Keep in mind that *you* were always the boss, and *you* hired your ego to work *for* you—no matter what your age or level of awareness.

Start by closing your eyes. Move to the time and place where you suspect you hired the ego to protect you from something or someone. Feel it and "see" it in your mind's eye. (If you believe you can't visualize, having a strong intention to receive the information will be just as effective. The imagination works with or without visuals.)

Write the job description as if you were back in that time, keeping in mind the purpose you intended in hiring your protector. Take this seriously. Make your final copy neat and *believe* in its purpose: this convinces your ego that you mean business and that you truly want change. Remember, *you're* the boss!

Use the following template when writing your original job description.

Original Job Template

Job Title: The name of your protector: choose something like Shy Girl, Rejecter, Critic, Queen, or Monster Kid.

Name and Title of Supervisor: Your name (or your nickname when you were a child, if that is more appropriate).

Department: Note the area of your life that was affected. For example, the department for Shy Girl might have been the Department of Introversion; she may have needed protection from verbal abuse, so she became a wallflower so as not to attract negative attention. The Rejecter's department was simply the Department of Rejection, because he rejected in return when he was constantly rejected himself. Monster Kid was so difficult that overly controlling and critical parents may have increased their control, usually to no avail. Maybe the Monster Kid's department was the Office of Obnoxiousness. Be creative with this—you might even have a laugh! Laughter is a great healer.

Pay Grade or Level: On a scale of 1 to 10, with 10 being the most important, write the job's level of importance to you at the time this job was created.

Type of Job: Full- or part-time—was this protection something that had to be active 24/7 or only in certain circumstances? Explain.

General Overview: Write a brief summary of the nature and purpose of the job, why you required protection—why you're hiring the protector.

Essential Functions: List the responsibilities and duties of your protector in order of importance, describing the ways you needed it to help you survive the situation. As an example, it may have protected you from tension in the home by helping you to hide out in your intellect as a high-achieving student.

Qualifications and Attributes: This is a list of what you would have asked your protector to do for you if it were an actual employee. This list doesn't need to make logical sense—you can be outrageous with it since you're contacting your historical self when you were a child, so it would reflect the way kids think.

Communication Skills: List the ways that you wanted your protector to communicate with you—through intuition, games and playing, dreams, physical feelings, or emotional signals, so that you could know it was there. This will come from a less conscious aspect of your memory, so trust your imagination—it's just as valuable as more conscious memory.

Other Skills, Mandatory and Preferred: For example, the ability to work longer than just at certain times or periods of your childhood if needed, and to continue to give you signals if you aren't paying attention, etc. These may come to you through recurring dreams.

Keep in mind that when your deep self originally designed this job, you had specific circumstances from which you needed protection. *Nothing* you did was in any way bad; you were *always* striving to be and express who you truly are. Also remember that you had long-term goals in mind at that time, not just your immediate needs. For example, if you were at risk of physical abuse and created a tough, mean-spirited demeanor as protection, your immediate goal might have been to remain safe, and your long-term goal might have been to come out alive and leave the environment when you could. This is where a precedent for life is set and why it's so hard to break patterns like these if we perceive them as victimization. The belief that we are still victims is actually a *judgment,* one that prevents movement toward resolution and transformation. What you experienced may have been devastating, painful, and traumatizing. The task here is not to deny your experience, but to use it as a way to awaken to your inherent strengths and purpose.

Take a moment to review and honor how the ego-protector served you in the past, and how that same service can be transformed into something the ego can support you with now.

Let's move on and give the protector a new job description.

Step 3: Creating Your New Job Description

Here you will transform the original job you gave your protector into a new job description, using the same template as before.

After completing this project, I suggest that you keep both the original and new job descriptions close by for the period of time it will take to imprint the new one upon your consciousness. Strike up a conscious dialogue with your ego-protector to reassure it that your purpose is not to destroy it, but rather to employ its power and energy in a new way that will serve you now. And very importantly, stay aware of all the subtle changes you sense or feel as you write the new job description.

New Job Description

Job Title: Shy Girl might become the Observer, who calmly reflects on situations before jumping in; the Rejecter could be transformed into the Screener, who stands back to consider all possibilities and make wise decisions; or Monster Kid could become the Energizer, who, like a battery, brings energy to you when needed. Keep in mind that this new job description is about an aspect that can serve your higher purpose *now*, rather than protecting a younger, less capable aspect of you. Remember that the new job must relate to the original job. Look for a job that is similar, using the same amount of energy and power as the original job had, but with new, positive action. It needs to support, empower, and free you, rather than protect you. If you skip this step, the process won't work. The energy involved in healing anything must at least meet, and preferably surpass, the energy of the original problem, situation, or aspect.

"Department": The area of your life it will affect, such as Creativity, Emotional Balance, or Harmonious Relationship.

Name and Title of Supervisor: Your name. You might inject a little humor here with your title, such as Boss Lady or Head Honcho.

"Pay" Grade or Level: The level of importance to you of this new way of being on a scale of 1 to 10, with 10 being the most important.

Type of Job: Full- or part-time: 24/7 or only when needed? Explain.

General Overview: Write a summary of the nature and purpose of the job—how you envision it working for you.

Essential Functions: List the responsibilities and duties in order of importance, and the ways it will assist you in your new perception of yourself and your life. How do you want its strength to serve you? How do you want it to reflect who you are when you are with others and with yourself?

Qualifications and Attributes: List the ways you want to feel after the ego accepts its new job, and things you want your protector to do for you, such as reminding you of your new way of being as you get used to it.

Communication Skills: Write down the way you want this aspect to communicate with you now, such as through intuition, dreams, physical or emotional signals, etc.

Other Skills, Mandatory and Preferred: List details of how you'd like this aspect to serve you in any way you haven't already mentioned. For example, the ability to give you signals if you aren't paying attention to the changes made.

As you complete the description, keep the following ideas in mind—these are *very important* to the success of this process:

You are the boss and you are hiring (activating) aspects of yourself—in this case, the ego-protector—to work *for* you. *You* are now and always have been responsible for your own life and all its aspects, responses, behaviors, feelings, and actions. All parts of your ego are your employees. The purpose in this process of writing a new job description is to develop a stronger sense of being in charge of your life as a creator rather than a victim.

Keep in mind the long-term goals noted in your original job description, not just your current needs; make sure this description will help you transform the old and vivify the new. Take command, but be careful not to create a battle between you and the protector—this will only trigger the old protections. Neither is this a practice of "making nice" with the ego. This is a balancing process where you clearly are in charge, but you are also willing to work with the protector as an ally.

Always keep your purpose in mind. Be aware of the influential whispers of old voices that are not your own. This will help you create the job description clearly, based upon what you want now and what you no longer need. Unless you allow them to remain active, Mom's and Dad's voices are just echoes of a time past. It's your choice.

As you review your new job description, be cautious of the ego's tendency to inflate its job's importance. Remember that it's trying to protect you and its authority over you, willingly given to it by your subconscious early in your life when you needed protection. Make it clear that it now has to adhere to what the *current and conscious* you wants and needs. If it is resistant, convince it that you are serious by reminding it that you're giving it a job *upgrade, not a demotion!*

Emphasize the scope and importance of this new job so this aspect of your ego will accept and maintain the job well. Keep in mind that what you are actually doing is transforming the *same* energy that composed the original ego-protector but with new ideals, beliefs, and confidence. You are using the same basic material, available to us all, and redesigning your intention, just like an architect remodels an old home.

It is important to understand that the foundation for the new job must be built upon the old. It is not a process of getting rid of anything—that's impossible. Both the old and new jobs must relate energetically. Transforming my Inner Critic involved upgrading to an Inner Discerner—same energy, different job, but related to the old one, the two jobs sharing similar energy and function.

By transforming the ego-protector, or any aspect of being, with respect and gratitude for what it has taught us, we are touched by the authentic essence of our Soul.

APPENDIX C
ALCHEMICAL ART PROJECTS

Engaging the imagination and the physical body with projects such as the ones in this appendix brings the power and mystery of the processes of alchemy into reality. Whenever we can bring dreams, feelings, thoughtforms, and desires up from the subconscious mind and out through our hands and eyes, we expand our perceptions. This is precisely why I use art in my classes in alchemy.

If our outer perceptions can be magnified and clarified by manipulating art materials, we can actually *see* a representation of what we have been studying intellectually and emotionally. It all begins to make more sense. And when outer perceptions are widened and deepened, our inner perceptions follow suit. By combining the work of alchemy with art, we are performing a sacred wedding of right- and left-brain functions, and integration of the conceptual and the graphic takes place as a result. Give yourself plenty of time to do these exercises—they work best if you do each one after you have completely worked each of the alchemical stages.

ALCHEMICAL ART PROJECT #1: CALCINATION
This Calcination exercise will assist you in understanding how the ego controls and limits your sense of happiness and freedom as it attempts to protect you from the various vicissitudes of life. The ego-protector continues to do this even when its maintenance of the status quo is no longer appropriate, beneficial, or necessary.

On black paper, use white or light-colored pencils or pastels to draw a circle in the center. This represents your ego. Now, as rapidly as possible, so as to "sabotage the saboteur"—the ego—as it tries to edit out the charged words, write words that describe how the ego influences your life. (Be careful that you don't see the ego as "the bad guy" here: whatever its activities have been in your life, they all had a purpose.) Put these words in smaller shapes (circles, squares, triangles, etc.) around the larger one, connecting them with lines to the center circle and to other related circles as they interconnect. Some will affect a few of the other words, and others will be connected to many. (Refer to the chart in Appendix A: The Gold Within You Process for a graphic example of this activity.)

After completing this Calcination project, imagine yourself as an alchemist working in your laboratory and burning the entire black paper as your first experiment. You can use an outdoor grill or metal container in which you can burn the paper. In a meditative state of mind, watch the paper burning, watch the fire as it consumes the paper, watch the flames and colors. Record your observations in your journal.

Finally, put the ashes in a clear glass bottle and cork it. Save this for the Dissolution exercise.

ALCHEMICAL ART PROJECT #2: DISSOLUTION

Here you will need watercolor paints and paper. Using your bottle of ashes from the Calcination project, pour out the ashes, add some water, and then mix in some watercolor paint(s). (Be careful not to add too much water—just enough to make a good paint consistency.) Use the colored ash paint to create a picture about your Dissolution process. Concentrate on expressing your watery aspects—your emotions, dreams, intuition, psychic awareness, creativity, the feminine, etc.

When it is dry, burn your painting and add its ashes to the ash bottle previously used at the end of your Calcination exercise. Just as with that exercise, meditatively watch your painting burn, then record your observations in your alchemy journal.

Alchemical Art Project #3: Separation

Write a poem or essay, or create a chart with lists of attributes of opposites that affect you. Add water to your bottle of ashes from your previous two projects. Mix some of this with paint colors and leave some as is. On heavy paper or poster board, paint a picture that expresses what the intellect, or rational mind, has revealed in regard to what must be separated—thoughts, beliefs, cherished ideas, attitudes, defenses—as no longer useful, needed, or appropriate. Once again, burn the painting in an alchemical ceremony, saving the ashes in your bottle for the next project. Record your experience in your journal.

Alchemical Art Project #4: Conjunction

Using paint, glue, stiff paper, poster board, or even thin (¹⁄₁₆") balsa wood, and the ashes from Separation as additional paint, create a sculpture that expresses the coming together, blending, harmonization, and sacred marriage of two seeming opposites within your life. This could be your masculine and feminine, shadow and light, conscious and unconscious, Heaven and Earth, etc. Burn this sculpture afterward and put the ashes in your bottle. Record your experiences in your journal.

Alchemical Art Project #5: Putrefaction-Fermentation

Use your choice of paper and paints, crayons, markers, colored pencils—whatever medium you like—and begin expressing death on the page, in whatever way you wish. It could be highly graphic or symbolic, abstract or representative. This painting is representative of the death of the old ways the ego served you. When you are finished, I recommend hanging it up someplace where you will see it often in order to allow its message to integrate. When you feel complete, burn your project and add its ashes to your bottle.

Alchemical Art Project #6: Distillation

Using silver lightweight poster board, create a painting or collage of your growing sense of spiritual connection. You may choose to use classic symbols, like angels or heavenly realms, or a more personal rendition of how you now perceive yourself spiritually. You will burn this project like the others, but this time put the ashes in a large bowl and add more water. Using an additional large bowl with cheesecloth tied across the top, run the ash water through the cheesecloth, then untie the cheesecloth and pour the water back into the first bowl. Rinse out the cheesecloth, and tie it back onto the bowl. Run the ash-water mixture back and forth between the two bowls, rinsing out the cloth each time, then adding clear water each time you pour the ash water. Continue to run the ash water through each bowl, over and over, always adding clear water, until the mixture runs clear. This will take time and patience, but Distillation takes time and patience, so use this as an true alchemical action. As you do this, keep the process of Distillation in mind. Store your clear, "distilled" water in your bottle. Write the experience in your journal.

Alchemical Art Project #7: Coagulation

Using gold lightweight poster board, and using your distilled water mixed with colored paints, create a picture or a collage of your perception of what it is like to be a coagulated, integrated, whole person. You may want to use items from nature, such as feathers, to depict birds or angels, leaves, flowers, etc. Open your heart as you create your piece, being aware of the crown of your head, and your connection to all of life. You may wish to do this in a meditative state or write in your journal to reflect on what you have learned and experienced in the seven stages of transformational alchemy. This project will not be burned, so don't forget that all the ashes from each stage are contained in this final project—it represents all aspects of you that you have transformed in the alchemical work you have done to discover and embody your inner gold.

ℛECOMMENDED READING

Bly, Robert. *A Little Book on the Human Shadow*. New York: Harper-One, 1988.

Edinger, Edward F. *Anatomy of the Psyche: Alchemical Symbolism in Psychotherapy*. Peru, IL: Open Court Publishing, 1985.

Goddard, David. *The Tower of Alchemy: An Advanced Guide to the Great Work*. York Beach, ME: Samuel Weiser, 1999.

Hauck, Dennis William. *The Emerald Tablet: Alchemy for Personal Transformation*. New York: Penguin Books, 1999.

———. *Sorcerer's Stone: A Beginner's Guide to Alchemy*. New York: Citadel Press, 2004.

Johnson, Robert A. *He: Understanding Masculine Psychology*. Harper Perennial, 1989.

———. *Owning Your Own Shadow: Understanding the Dark Side of the Psyche*. New York: HarperCollins, 1993.

_____. *She: Understanding Feminine Psychology*. Harper Perennial, 1989.

_____. *We: Understanding the Psychology of Romantic Love*. Harper-One, 1985.

Joy, W. Brugh, MD. *Avalanche: Heretical Reflections on the Dark and the Light*. New York: Ballantine Books, 1990.

Marlan, Stanton. *The Black Sun: The Alchemy and Art of Darkness*. College Station, TX: Texas A&M University Press, 2005.

Moore, Thomas. *Dark Nights of the Soul: A Guide to Finding Your Way Through Life's Ordeals*. New York: Penguin Books, 2004.

Newton, Michael, PhD. *Destiny of Souls: New Case Studies of Life Between Lives.* Saint Paul, MN: Llewellyn Publishing, 2000.

———. *Journey of Souls: Case Studies of Life Between Lives.* Saint Paul, MN: Llewellyn Publishing, 1994.

Raff, Jeffrey. *Jung and the Alchemical Imagination.* York Beach, ME: Samuel Weiser, 2000.

Schwartz, Robert. *Your Soul's Plan: Do We Plan Our Life Challenges Before Birth?* Berkeley, CA: Frog Books, 2009.

von Franz, Marie-Louise. *Alchemy: An Introduction to the Symbolism and the Psychology.* Toronto, Canada: Inner City Books, 1980.

Whitton, Joel L., MD. *Life Between Life.* New York: Warner Books, 1986.

To Contact the Author

If you wish to contact the author or would like more information about this book, please write to the author in care of Llewellyn Worldwide Ltd. and we will forward your request. Both the author and publisher appreciate hearing from you and learning of your enjoyment of this book and how it has helped you. Llewellyn Worldwide Ltd. cannot guarantee that every inquiry can be answered, but all will be forwarded to the author. Dr. Shanderá prefers to respond to inquiries via e-mail and requests that readers include their e-mail address. Please write to:

Nanci Shanderá, PhD
℅ Llewellyn Worldwide
2143 Wooddale Drive
Woodbury, MN 55125-2989

Many of Llewellyn's authors have websites with additional information and resources. For more information, please visit our website at http://www.llewellyn.com.